ANCIENT NORTH-EAST INDIA
(PRĀGJYOTISHA)
A PAN-INDIA PERSPECTIVE

ANCIENT NORTH-EAST INDIA
(PRĀGJYOTISHA)
A PAN-INDIA PERSPECTIVE

(Up to Seventh Century AD)

AJAY MITRA SHASTRI

ARYAN BOOKS INTERNATIONAL
NEW DELHI

Ancient North-East India (Prāgjyotisha) : A Pan-India Perspective

ISBN-81-7305-219-0

Published in **2002** by :
ARYAN BOOKS INTERNATIONAL
Pooja Apartments, 4B, Ansari Road, Darya Ganj, New Delhi-110002 (India)
Tel.: 3287589, 3255799; Fax: 91-11-3270385; E-mail : aryanbooks@vsnl.com

Computer Typeset at Welcome Computers, New Delhi
Printed in India at B.B.N. Printers, New Delhi

To

my esteemed friend

DR SWARAJYA PRAKASH GUPTA

an eminent archaeologist and art historian

who has been taking keen interest in and

encouraging me for more and more academic work,

as a token of love, regards and admiration

PREFACE

The present monograph has emerged from the lectures delivered on 6-8 April 1999 at the North-Eastern Hill University (NEHU), Shillong, under the celebrated Professor H.K. Barpujari Lecture series.

When I was invited to deliver this prestigious series of lectures it was suggested in view of my known interest and specialisation and the stipulations of the series that I might speak on some inscriptional aspects. I collected the data from all the available inscriptions, which are quite revealing, but felt that it would be far more interesting and absorbing to speak on some more appealing aspects. And I was taken aback by the oft-repeated myth that the people of North-Eastern India were, by and large, racially and culturally different from those of the rest of the country. And I felt that exploding this myth would not only be more rewarding as the topic of my lectures but would also serve the much more useful object of making the people realise that historically and culturally they are one with the rest of their fellow countrymen despite the obvious and natural regional differences which are quite normal in such a vast country as undivided India was. In fact, the absence of such differences would have adversely told on the talent and receptivity of the people. Accordingly I chose for these lectures a re-look at the region's past in a pan-Indian perspective.

It is often stated and the common people made to believe by constantly harping that the people of what was anciently called Prāgjyotisha and the surroundings were away from the mainstream of Indian life and culture, and that the Āryans attempted to colonise them and impose on them their alien culture. But it has been demonstrated with strong evidence that the word *Ārya* was without any racial or linguistic connotation and that in ancient India it was employed in a purely cultural sense. It was given, most probably deliberately, a racial sense by the Europeans with a vested interest to sow the seeds of dissension among their subject people and perpetuate their rule. And from the earliest recorded times we find that the people of the North-East and those of the rest of the country were aware of and had a close interaction with one another. And with the passage of time these contacts and bonds grew more and more intimate and the region in question and the rest of the country contributed to the common cultural development enriching each other. Thus the monograph seeks to trace chronologically and in a pan-Indian perspective the politico-cultural contacts that the region had with the rest of the Indian people.

The region covered in this monograph includes the present state of Assam and the states recently carved out of it, viz. Meghalaya, Mizoram, Nagaland and Arunachal Pradesh, as well as, to some extent, Manipur. Almost the whole of this North-Eastern region was then loosely known as Prāgjyotisha which is a much more appropriate nomenclature inasmuch as it has the virtue of being sanctified by a hallowed age-old tradition. It must, of course, be remembered that not much evidence has surfaced from the last four states carved out of Assam for want of archaeological explorations and excavations.

The work consists of three chapters. The inaugural chapter dwells upon what may be summarily called early historical phase and covers the period up to the Maurya age ending with the commencement of the second century BC. It deals with the preliminary issues like the nomenclature and pertinent references from Pāṇini's grammatical work *Ashṭādhyāyī*, the early Buddhist canonical literature including the Jātaka and Tripiṭaka texts, the *Rāmāyaṇa* and *Mahābhārata*, and Kauṭilya's *Arthaśāstra*, to mention only the most prominent texts, which shed quite a lurid light on the life and culture of Prāgjyotisha and its abiding relations with the rest of what was known as Bhāratavarsha. It has been pointed out that though as of now there is no definite allusion to it in any part of the Vedic literature, there is every likelihood of the Vedic people's familiarity with it. It has also been demonstrated that despite normal mixture of racial and cultural elements from extra-Indian regions, the predominant feature was its oneness with India, both culturally and physically.

The next chapter takes stock of the evidence from about the second century BC to the sixth century AD, that is, roughly speaking, from the age of the Śuṅgas to the pre-Bhāskaravarman period. To begin with, it has been demonstrated with the help of recent archaeological findings at Vadagokugiri (popularly called Bhaitbārī) in the district of Tura in West Garo hills in the present state of Meghalaya that the prevalence and prosperity of the Indian religious systems in the Prāgjyotisha region are archaeologically documented at least from about the beginning of the Christian era, if not earlier. We have shown that as of now there is nothing to prove that this region was invaded by Pushyamitra Śuṅga. Foreign visitors' and writers' notices have also been discussed, albeit in brief, which also reveal close commercial and cultural relations of the region with rest of India. What is most pertinent to note is that all these descriptions are part of their account of India, which shows that they treated the region as a part of the Indian subcontinent. The Bhauma-Nāraka or Varman dynasty is known archaeologically to have come to prominence about the beginning of the second quarter of the fourth century AD and thereafter it grew gradually leaps and bounds. We have demonstrated basing on the evidence of the Nālandā seals of the famous and last known Prāgjyotisha king Bhāskaravarman and of that attached to his Dūbī plates that a personage named Naraka was the father of Pushyavarman, the first historically known member of this dynasty. Its members were staunch adherents of Vedic-Paurāṇic religious systems and in addition to themselves performing some of the Vedic rituals ensured the entrenchment of Vedic culture and learning by making land-grants to learned brāhmaṇas and thereby creating powerful and prosperous settlements called *agrāhāras* which contributed enormously to the spread of literacy and learning among the people. Their following Vedic religion, of course, did not come in the way of their revering great teachers of other religious sects, and we have strong evidence, if such an evidence were needed, in Kalhaṇa's *Rāja-taraṅgiṇī* to show that a member of this dynasty revered a renowned Buddhist pontiff from Tibet so much as to be called his *guru* (spiritual teacher) and to mislead some modern historians into postulating the theory of the popularity of Buddhism in Prāgjyotisha in those days despite the searching eye of the Chinese pilgrim Yuan Chwang not only not finding anything Buddhistic in the region but also telling us that whatever Buddhists might be there performed their religious rites in secrecy.

The growth of political power aided by industrial development resulting into great economic prosperity laid the strong foundations on which Bhāskaravarman raised a political superstructure which forms the theme of the last chapter. He came to power at a very critical time but by dint of astute diplomacy and foresight, not to speak of military strength, was not only able to ward off the powerful enemy but also to carve out an extensive eastern Indian empire and to play a vital role on a pan-Indian plane. He had a great friend in Harsha Śīlāditya who was the greatest Indian monarch of the period, and both participated in the momentous religious assemblies that have been made well-known by the Chinese pilgrim Yuan Chwang who was a great friend of both these great Indians of the time as well as his biographer Shaman Hwui Li. He is also reported to have aided the Chinese adventurers following Harsha's demise and the usurpation of his kingdom by one of his ministers. He was also probably a keen student of philosophy and a good Sanskrit scholar and, according to the Chinese sources, requested for a Sanskrit rendering of the well-known Chinese philosopher Lao-tse's work. We do not know if he actually received the Sanskrit version though there exists some evidence that attempts in this direction were made in China.

We have tried to remove the erroneous notion prevailing among some historians that king Avantivarman named in the concluding stanza in some of the manuscripts of the famous political drama *Mudrā-Rākshasa* was the son and immediate successor of Bhāskaravarman. We have evidence that the Bhauma-Kara kings of Orissa were an offshoot of the Bhaumas of Prāgjyotisha.

Our discussion terminates with the end of the seventh century AD. But there is enough evidence to show that the relations between Prāgjyotisha and the rest of India continued and grew more and more intimate with the passage of time and we have numerous enlightening references in inscriptions that reveal that numerous learned brāhmaṇas came to Prāgjyotisha from other parts of India and those from Kāmarūpa, which had already turned into a great centre of Vedic culture, went to other parts of the Indian sub continent.

The delineation in these pages is naturally restricted as regards spatial extent by the accessibility of evidence, literary as well as archaeological, and the extant data mostly, though unfortunately, appertain the plains with just a sprinkling of archaeological material in the adjoining Garo hill region of Meghalaya. We are confident, however, that intense fieldwork in the other regions, as and when undertaken seriously, will certainly afford evidence similar to that in Meghalaya which was thrown up by a very small-scale digging. We only wish that such a search is undertaken in other areas also sooner than later.

Prachi, 23 Vidya Vihar
Rana Pratap Nagar
Nagpur – 440 022

Ajay Mitra Shastri

CONTENTS

ACKNOWLEDGEMENTS

Such a work is just inconceivable without the spontaneous help and co-operation from others, and I was fortunate enough to receive these in an ample measure from different quarters. First of all, I am grateful to the University authorities for inviting me to deliver this prestigious series of lectures which afforded me an opportunity to divert and devote my attention to the North-East. And this would just have not been possible without the enlightened initiative of Professor Jai Prakash Singh, Department of History, North-Eastern Hill University, Shillong, who broached the suggestion and ensured its implementation by supplying much of the material inaccessible to me as well as by constantly goading and encouraging me in moments of diffidence. He offered some highly valuable suggestions which have helped me considerably. It is no exaggeration to concede that these lectures owe their inception to him and I miss words adequate enough to vent my heartfelt thanks to him. Unfortunately, he could not remain present during my lectures due to certain unavoidable reasons.

To the Pro-Vice Chancellor of the University I am thankful for presiding over the first lecture and to Professor J.B. Bhattacharya, then Vice Chancellor of the Cachhar University, for inaugurating the lecture series. By my good fortune Professor Dr Kumar Suresh Singh, formerly Director General, Anthropological Survey of India and then Rajiv Professor of Anthropology at the University, was present at Shillong at the time and chaired the remaining two lectures and offered some highly useful scholarly suggestions in his concluding remarks.

I am highly thankful to Professor Imdad Hussain, Head of the Department of History, North-Eastern Hill University, who extended all the courtesies in an ample measure during my stay at the University Guest House at Shillong. His colleagues in the Department, more particularly Drs. David Reid Syiemlieh and F.A. Qadri, also deserve my sincere thanks for courtesies and help in various ways.

Sincere appreciation and thanks are due Dr Subodh Kumar Mitra, Superintending Archaeologist, Prehistory Branch, Archaeological Survey of India, Nagpur, for taking affectionate immediate care of my needs of library and the provision of photographs illustrating the book. The whole illustrated material has been brought to light by Shri A.K. Sharma, formerly of the Archaeological Survey of India, who conducted the small-scale but highly rewarding archaeological excavations at Vadagokugiri. It is different though that, as will be seen from some of the captions, I differ from him as regards certain identifications. The photographs have been prepared from the original material preserved at the Prehistory Branch of the Archaeological Survey of India under the personal supervision of Dr Mitra. Professor Chandrashekhar Gupta, Head, Dept. of Ancient Indian History, Culture and Archaeology, Nagpur University, also was, as usual, of great help in various ways including some of the photographs. Dr M.I. Quddusi, Director (Arabic and Persian Epigraphy), Archaeological Survey of India, Nagpur, supplied on request earliest references to the name Assam in mediaeval Persian chronicles for which I am very grateful. Shri J.N. David, Librarian, Archaeological Survey of India, Nagpur, also has been of great help and issued whichever books I needed.

Shri Vikas Arya of the Aryan Books International, New Delhi, took keen enlightened interest in publishing the book so very neatly for which he deserves heartfelt thanks.

Ajay Mitra Shastri

ABBREVIATIONS

CA	*The Classical Age*, Vol. III of *HCIP*, eds. R.C. Majumdar and A.D. Pusalkar
CAI	*The Classical Accounts of India*, ed. R.C. Majumdar
CHA	*A Cultural History of Assam*, I, by B.K. Barua
EHK	*Early History of Kāmarūpa* by K.L. Barua
EI	*Epigraphia Indica*
HCESA	*Harsha-Charita : Eka Sāṁskṛitika Adyayana (Hindi)* by Vasudev Sharan Agrawala
HCIP	Bharatiya Vidya Bhavan's *History and Culture of the Indian People*
HCPA	*The History of the Civilisation of the People of Assam* by P.C. Choudhury
IA	*Indian Antiquary*
IAA	*Inscriptions of Ancient Assam* by M.M. Sharma
IC	*Indian Culture*
IHQ	*The Indian Historical Quarterly*
ISKMD	*India as Seen in the Kuṭṭanī-mata of Dāmodaragupta* by Ajay Mitra Shastri
JARS	*The Journal of Assam Research Society*
JASB	*The Journal of the Asiatic Society of Bengal*
JBORS	*The Journal of the Bihar and Orissa Research Society*
JPASB	*The Journal and Proceedings of the Asiatic Society of Bengal*
JRAS	*The Journal of the Royal Asiatic Society of Great Britain and Ireland*
JRASB	*The Journal of the Royal Asiatic Society of Bengal*
JRASBL	*Journal of the Asiatic Society of Bengal*, letters.
KŚ	*Kāmarūpa-śāsanāvali*, ed. Dimbeswar Sharma
SEHA	*Studies in the Early History of Assam* by K.L. Barua

ILLUSTRATIONS

(All the non-epigraphic illustrations refer to the excavated finds from Bhaitbari, Meghālaya)

Chapter I

EARLY HISTORICAL PHASE

1. Introductory
   - Nomenclature
     - Assam
     - Prāgjyotisha
     - Kāmarūpa
2. 'Tribalism' and 'Āryanisation'
3. Early Contacts
   - Vedic Period
   - Pāṇini's *Ashṭādhyāyī*
   - Early Buddhist Canonical Literature
   - The Epics: *Rāmāyaṇa* and *Mahābhārata*
   - The Maurya Age

1. INTRODUCTORY

Before we proceed with our historical survey of the theme, it is imperative to dwell upon some preliminaries which are a *sine qua non* for providing a proper perspective for the appreciation of and have an important bearing on the subject under treatment.

NOMENCLATURE

Assam

Most of the region forming the theme of these lectures was till recently known as Assam and a major part of it is still called by this name. This name is, however, not met with in ancient sources, either literary or inscriptional, dating earlier than the sixteenth century AD. To our knowledge the name is for the first time referred to as Ashām by Abul Fazl, a great scholarly protégé of the Mughal emperor Akbar, in his well-known work *Ain-i-Akbari*.[1] The name is also employed by Ami Ahmadn Razi, another chronicler of the same period, in his *Haft Iqlim*.[2] The name Asam is also met with in the *Pādshāhnāmā*, a chronicle of the time of the Mughal emperor Shāh Jahān by his courtier Abdul Hamid Lauhorī, and in the *Alamgīrnāmā*, a chronicle of the reign of emperor Alamgīr, better known as Aurangzeb , by Muhammad Kazim,[3] and in the form Asem in the travelogue of the famous traveller Tavernier.[4] The mediaeval Muslim writers are also familiar with the name Kāmrūp which is the nomenclature encountered in all the earlier Persian chronicles. In so far as the Assamese literature is concerned, the name is first met with in the *Guru-charita* of Daityāri Ṭhākur of the sixteenth or early seventeenth century AD, but for the Ahom people. It is somewhat later that Sīryakhari Daivajña in his *Darang-raja-vaṁśāvali* employs it as the name of both the Ahoms as well as the upper Assam valley.[5]

The name Assam is actually an anglicised form of the earlier Indian (or Assamese) formation *Asama* which owes its origin, according to the popular notion, to the Tāi or Shān people of Siamese-Chinese branch of the Sino-Tibetan extraction called Ahoms who immigrated to the upper Brahmaputra valley by way of North Burmā through the course of the river Noā Dihing and started on their career as the rulers of this region during thirteenth century AD. They first entered the region in AD 1228 under the leadership of Chaolung Sue-ka-phā, a Tāi prince of Mueng Mao, who was brought up at Hsen-se, the capital of Maolung, by his maternal grandmother.[6] Though they came as invaders and established their rule over the region which lasted several centuries (up to AD 1838), they made it their home and patronised and adopted its life-style, religion and culture. In fact, they became one with the local populace and, though undoubtedly present, can hardly be distinguished from them at present.[7]

There is, however, a great divergence of opinion about the origin of this name. The Ahoms were a tribe belonging to the Siāmese Shān race and called themselves Tāi. In fact, the Tāi did not call themselves Ahoms. According to the popular Ahom tradition, at the time when they invaded the region, the local people called them ***asama*** (unparalleled or peerless) because of their superb fighting abilities and later reconciliation and this name was later applied to the region conquered by them.[8] According to the well-known linguist Suniti Kumar Chatterji, 'The original form of the word in Old Burmese was *Rham* or *Hyam* which became in Middle Burmese (after AD 1050) *Yham* and *Hyam*, and then in different languages *Aham, Ahom, Cyam, am, Syam, Siam,* Syāma, *Asama, Asam, Shan*, etc.'[9] B.K. Kakati, on the other hand, thinks that this tradition is later and that ***Asama*** may represent a later Sanskritisation of the earlier form ***Āchām*** which may mean 'unconquered,' or 'undefeated', for in the Ahom or Tāi dialect, ***chām*** means 'to defeat', and with the Assamese prefix ***ā*** (in the negative sense) it would get a negative meaning.[10] But according to another, though much less probable, view,[11] the name (Āsām) is most probably traceable to the Boḍo word Hā-com meaning the low or level country.[12] Thus while some scholars champion the view that the regional name was derived from that of the people, the adoption of the last theory would mean just the reverse, viz. the Ahoms were so called after the region. Grierson has pointed out that ***Shān*** is the Burmese corruption of the original Siāmese word *Shām*.[13] Following it, it is possible to suggest that the name Shān or Shām or *Ashān* was the basis of the modern name Assam.[14]

The foregoing summary of the current views is enough to show that they all are purely speculative and there is no finality about the origin of the name Assam except that it has something to do with the people's name, viz. Ahom, or some topographical features of the region. We therefore feel free to hazard yet another suggestion. Just as the sibilant changes, in some dialects, into *h*, so also it is possible conversely for *h* to get transformed into *s*, and so the name Asama may have been derived from the Ahom people. And the current form of the name with duplication of the sibilant (Āssām) is only an anglicised form of the original *Asama*. But we must remember that the Tāis never use the name Ahom for themselves and continue the nomenclature of Tāi. It is therefore more reasonable to regard the name as based on some other fact. It might have been derived from the name of the country through which the Tāis reached India, Shān or Shyām, by which Thailand is commonly known to Indians.

Another possibility must also not be ignored in this context. The regional names in the North-East are sometimes found based on some topographical features, and the name Samataṭa ('country comprising even coastline') met with in the Allahabad pillar inscription of the Gupta emperor Samudra Gupta and other later sources is an example in point. It is not impossible therefore that the original form of the name was Asama which denoted an 'uneven' or 'rough' land, and it has nothing to do with the Ahom people who might have derived their own name from it. This is just a conjecture and must be taken for what it is. It must, of course, be admitted that the name is not found employed in any early work which is only an *argumentum ex silentio* and need not be taken seriously.

The area of this undivided state of Assam (before it was split into a number of states in recent times in different years) lay between latitudes 28° 18' and 24° North and longitudes 89° 46' and 97° 4' East. It comprised an area of about 54,000 square miles including 24,283 square miles of the plain region of the Brahmaputra valley and some 19,500 of southern and northern hill tracts. It is bordered on the north by the sub-Himalayan ranges of Bhutan, Aka, Dafala, Miri, Abar and Mishmi which are the names derived from those of the people inhabiting them. Its eastern boundary is formed by a spur of the Āssām range of the Himālayas known as Pāṭkāi, on the south-east by the Naga hills on the Burmese border, on the south by the Lushai hills touching the borders of Burma, on the south-east by the Hill Tippera and Mymensingh, while it borders Tibet on the north which forms a bone of contention between India and China. The western border is formed by the Garo Hills and the river Soṅkosha dividing it from Bengal.[15] This was the natural geographical spread of Āssām though, naturally enough, its political borders changed, shrunk or extended with its fluctuating political fortunes. As will be apparent, its topography was varied: some areas were watered by rivers and were very fertile and plain, while others were mountainous though rich in animal, mineral and other natural products. Generally speaking, all this region covered by the un-partitioned state of Assam as well as the North-Eastern Frontier Agency (NEFA) which is now constituted by the truncated states of Arunachal, Assam, Meghalaya, Mizoram and Nagaland as well as Manipur (to some extent) forms the subject-matter of our treatment. It must be conceded though that in view of the availability of profuse epigraphical wealth, the Brahmaputra valley has naturally claimed much greater attention. At the times of imperial rulers like the traditional Bhagadatta and historically documented Bhāskaravarman, all these regions partook of their impact even though they did not in reality form part of a common political and cultural denominator owing to their natural, racial and cultural diversities which found an adequate place and scope for expression. The inclusion of all this area into the conceptual sphere of influence, even if not in the kingdom, of Prāgjyotisha is evidenced by the description in the Great Epic that the armies of Bhagadatta comprised, *inter alia*, the Chīnas and the mountaineers. The whole of this region, which forms the north-eastern part of India now, is situated roughly between 22 and 29 28' northern latitudes and 89 40' and 97 22' eastern longitudes.

With the political consolidation of this region by the British, the following definite form of territorial groupings with definite form and boundaries emerged:

1. The Garos, Khasis and the Jaintias in the hills of identical names;
2. the Assamese in the Brahmaputra valley;
3. plains tribes in the west of the valley, specially in its upper and northern parts;
4. the Mishmis, Miris, Daflas and Abors in the north-eastern part;
5. the Naga tribal groups in the Naga hills;
6. the Metheis of Manipur;
7. Mizos as well as the Lakhars, Pawis, etc., in the Lushai hills; and
8. tribal Tripurites in the north-eastern parts of Tripura.[16]

Prāgjyotisha

In earlier inscriptions and literature the region is found mentioned as Prāgjyotisha or Kāmarūpa. The former name is much older and popular than the latter[17] and continued in use till a very late date, specially in the epigraphs of the local rulers who prided in styling themselves as *Prāgjyotish-eśvara* or *Prāgjyotish-ādhipati,* 'lord of Prāgjyotisha'. It comprehended a much larger area than the other name and included not only Assam and perhaps some of the hilly regions on the north-east but also a considerable portion of Bengal. F.E. Pargiter had an inflated notion about the extent of the early kingdom of Prāgjyotisha which in his opinion comprised not only a major portion of Assam but also the Jalpaiguri, Coochbihar, Rangpur, Bogra, Mymensiṅgh, Dhaka and Tippera districts and some part of the Pabna district of Bengal (much of this region is now included in Baṅgladesh) as well as probably eastern part of Nepal.[18] According to him, generally speaking, Prāgjyotisha 'comprised the whole of North Bengal proper'.[19] Some historians go even beyond it and hold that its western boundary was formed by the river Kosi and that the Purnea district of Bihar formed a part of this kingdom.[20] However, the untenability of these views is apparent from the fact that North Bengal was actually known as Puṇḍra or Puṇḍravardhana-*bhukti* which was quite distinct from Prāgjyotisha and bordered it on the west.[21] The *Mārkaṇḍeya-purāṇa* (Kūrmavibhāga, Ch. LVIII) and Varāhamihira's *Bṛihatsaṁhitā* (XIV. 23, 31) place it in the eastern division of Bhāratavarsha.[22] Its capital was called Prāgjyotishapura which was situated close to the present-day Guwāhāṭī and the name is now represented in that of the village Dispur, two miles south of Guwahati.[23]

As for the genesis of this name, the *Kālikā-purāṇa*, dating from about the tenth century AD, avers that formerly staying here god Brahmā created stars in consequence whereof the city came to be designated as Prāgjyotisha-pura.[24] This tradition is sought to be substantiated by some scholars who find support for it in the presence of a Navagraha temple on a hill called Chitrāchala near (to the east of) Guwahati which might have been responsible for the name of Prāgjyotisha-pura.[25] They also invite our attention to a number of Assamese manuscripts on astrology and astronomy and the prevalence of the solar and fire worship in early Assam and the *Bihu* festival associated with fire worship and fertility rites and the astronomical significance of the region.[26] Others reject this tradition and propose to connect it with the topographical features like its situation in a hilly region which is, most probably, denoted by an Austric formation such as *Pagar-juh(jo)-tich(chāchh)* denoting a region of extensive high hills which may have later been Sanskritised as Prāgjyotisha.[27] Still others connect the name with the Chinese immigrants and feel that the Chao Zuthis migrating to India were called Zuthis and those coming to Assam came to be known as Prāg Zuthis ('eastern Zuthis') who provided the basis for the Sanskrit name Prāgjyotisha.[28]

It is apparent that there has been a free play of fancy about the origin of this name and the suggestions are more often than not fraught with contradictions.[29] It is not unlikely, however, that the region got this name because of the earlier sunrise here as compared to the other regions of India, *prāg* meaning *before* or *earlier* and *jyotisha* referring to the most important astronomical phenomenon, viz. sun. Alternatively, *prāg* may be taken in the sense of 'east' and the name may denote the 'land of eastern sunrise' or the 'eastern land of sunrise'.

Kāmarūpa

The name Kāmarūpa occurs for the first time, in so far as epigraphy is concerned, in the Allahabad pillar inscription of the Gupta emperor Samudra Gupta dating from about mid-fourth century AD which mentions its king as one of the rulers of the states that bordered on his empire (*pratyanta-nṛipati*).[30] In case the renowned Sanskrit poet-dramatist Kālidāsa is placed in the first century BC as averred by tradition, the antiquity of the name may go back a few centuries earlier. Describing Raghu's *digvijaya,* he states that on his crossing the river Lauhitya (Brahmaputra) the lord of Prāgjyotisha (*Prāgjyotish-eśvara*) trembled with fear being unable to resist his armies and he (*Kāmarūp-eśvara*, 'the lord of Kāmarūpa') presented him with numerous rutting elephants and the shadow of his feet on a golden stool.[31] It will be obvious from a perusal of these stanzas that Kālidāsa has employed the names Prāgjyotisha and Kāmarūpa as synonymous.[32] Sanskrit lexicographers including Yādavaprakāśa (*Vaijayantī*), Hemachandra (*Abhidhāna-chintāmaṇi*, p. 381) and Purushottama (*Trikāṇḍa-śesha*, p. 93) also treat the two names as of an identical connotation.[33] The name Kāmarūpa figures in varied contexts in, *inter alia,* the *Mārkaṇḍeya-purāṇa*, the *Garuḍa-purāṇa*, the *Daśa-kumāra-charita* of Daṇḍin, the *Kāvya-mīmāṁsā* and *Karpūra-mañjarī* of Rājaśekhara, the *Vikramāṅkadeva-charita* of the Kashmirī poet Bilhaṇa, the *Rāma-charita* of Sandhyākaranandin and the *Rāja-taraṅgiṇī* of Kalhaṇa, in so far as the non-Assamese literary sources are concerned, sometimes along with Prāgyotisha. The Chinese traveller Yuan Chwang of the seventh century AD and the Arabic writer Abū Raihān ibn Muhammad, better known as Al-berunī, also speak of Kāmarūpa and the former supplies, as will be seen in the sequel, a very valuable piece of information of a historical nature. Of the epigraphs from outside, besides the aforesaid Allahābād pillar inscription of Samudra Gupta which records the oldest epigraphical allusion, the name Kāmarūpa is met with in, *inter alia*, a grant of the Gaṅga king Avantivarman, the Paśchimbāg grant of the Chandra king Śrīchandra, the Belwā grant of Bhojavarman, the Deopārā inscription of the Sena king Vijayasena and the Mādhainagar grant of the last Sena king Lakshmaṇasena.[34] What is most surprising to note in the present context is the fact that while the name Kāmarūpa became more popular than the other older name Prāgjyotisha in other regions, in Assam itself the latter was much more popular and, as pointed out earlier, most of the Āssāmese kings styled themselves *Prāgjyotish-eśvara* or *Prāgjyotish-ādhipati* in their own epigraphical records which are fairly numerous. And it is only in some rather late inscriptions and some later texts, especially with a high Tāntrik orientation, like the *Kālikā-purāṇa*, the *Yoginī-tantra* and the *Hara-Gaurī-saṁvāda* that the name Kāmarūpa together with the connected myths is met with. These works give a rather inflated extent of the area included in Kāmarūpa. The *Yoginī-tantra* (XI. 16-18), for instance, defines its limits as follows:

> From the Kāñchana mountain of Nepala up to the confluence of the Brahmaputra and from the Karatoyā river to Dikkaravāsinī its northern boundary is formed by Kañjagiri and the western one by the river Karatoyā, the eastern one by the Dikshu, river and on the south the confluence of the Brahmaputra and the Lākshā is known everywhere as the extent of Kāmarūpa.[35] The same text gives the extent of Kāmarūpa as thirty *yojanas* in breadth and a hundred *yojanas* in length.[36]

This indeed is the greatest possible extent of Kāmarūpa, though it differed from time to time, and one need not be misled by it into believing that it was true of all the periods of its chequered annals. In fact, originally the name was applied to a small tract around the present city of Guwahati and included the renowned temple of Kāmākhyā, but with the territorial aggrandisement of its rulers, fresh territories were annexed and its geographical limits got expanded considerably.

The Purāṇic legends account for the origin of the name by associating it with Kāmadeva, the Indian cupid and god Śiva. It is believed that Kāma was deputised, by the gods with the object of luring god Śiva to sexual and resulting procreative activity when the latter was averse to the worldly life because of his mourning the sad demise of his spouse Satī, but the former was reduced to ashes by his angry third eye. But later by Śiva's proverbial grace he recovered his original form (*rūpa*). The scene of this episode is laid here, and this is said to have given the country the name under reference. The popularity of the Kāmākhyā goddess and the associated Tāntric ritual throughout the country naturally contributed to its renown and overshadowed the earlier name Prāgjyotisha. And the whole phenomenon is a mirror to the tremendous growth in the widespread acceptance of the cult.

But most of the scholars are naturally not willing to concede this traditional origin of the name and attempt to account for it otherwise. The indefatiguable Chatterji S.K. prefers to treat these names as of a Boḍo extraction and as representing a tribal name prior to their becoming associated with localities. He feels that the prefix *Kam* or *Kām* forms an element occurring in the name of the westernmost tribe of the Boḍos, viz. the *Koches* (modern *Koṁch, Koch,* from an earlier **Kawoṁcha* or **Kamocha*, Sanskritised into *Kamboja* in the tenth century AD).[36] B.K. Kakati treats this name as of an Austric origin as also the names Kāmatā and Kamilā (present Komilla in Bangladesh). He connects it with Austric words like Kāmru and *Kāmrut*, the Santālī names of a minor divinity.[37] It is no doubt true that several feminine cults and fertility rites, developed as well as primitive, must have contributed to the formation and growth of the Kāmākhyā cult as finalised as is the case with several other Indian cults. It is quite likely that some primitive goddesses were merged into and identified with some dominating goddess and the same merger and equations must have marked the religious beliefs and practices in question. And as it was a common process in ancient India and continues to this day, there is nothing absolutely to be surprised about it in this case alone.

2. 'TRIBALISM' AND 'ĀRYANISATION'

By its very geographical situation at the north-eastern end of India and hemmed in between the rest of India on the west and Myanmar and Bhutan and Tibet (now forming part of China) on the east and north respectively, North-Eastern India naturally received an influx of people together with their life-styles and ideas from all these areas from times immemorial. Thus, in the population of this region scholars have noticed the Boḍos (including the Koch, the Kachhāri, the Lalung, the Dimachha, the Garo, the Rabha, the Tipura, the Chutiya, the Maran and the Mech[38] groups) generally regarded as belonging to the Tibeto-Burman race and much more numerous and stronger than others and with much greater contributions to the Assamese culture, and the Shāns or Tāis (including the Ahoms who are very prominent and probably givers of the name Assam as seen above, the Khamtis, the Pahakiyals, the Naras and the Aitonityas who followed the Ahoms).[39] Several anthropologists have detected among the people diverse racial elements like Negrito, Austric-Asiatic, Mongolian and what are called Alpine-Āryan as well as the admixture of all these and other races. Some have also traced the Nagas from the Dravidians who first went from South India to Burma by sea and thence to Assam. In these matters there is such a wide difference of opinion and free play of imagination that it is just impossible to be sure on any point.[40] The only certain thing is that there were several immigrations, sometimes in waves after waves, from most of these areas. Although there is a persistent shade of opinion advocating that the immigration from east and north preceded that from the west by a very long stretch of time,[41] the very fact that while the latter region has no strong physical barrier and could access the region as much as other plain regions without any difficulty while those in other directions had to negotiate the rather difficult mountainous barriers which proved a great problem even in later times[42] should suffice to establish that the close contacts and interaction with the former region must have existed from very early times.[43] And it is vouched for by the fact that the general life in this region, more especially in the plains, is under the impact of Vedic-Purāṇic ideas and rituals and we have explicit evidence of the intimate knowledge of this region and its inhabitants in the form of indubitable references from very early known times, whereas there is none from the other side. And what is even more interesting is that the former show awareness of even differences in general physical appearance of the residents[44] of this region, and it is with these dissimilarities that they were accepted as an inseparable part of the general Indian society.

A majority of inhabitants[45] of North-Eastern India are generally regarded as tribals with varying levels of development. Some of them are believed to be still in the most primitive stage and are looked at with disdain. The term 'tribe' has been coined by anthropologists to describe human groups with a low stage of development. In the *Oxford Wordpower Dictionary* (1993, p. 662) it is defined as 'a group of people that have the same language and customs and that are ruled by a chief or chiefs'. In the new edition (1987) of the *Longman's Dictionary of Contemporary English* (p. 1133) it is said to denote 'a social group made up of people of the same race, beliefs, customs, language, etc., living in a particular area under the leadership of a chief'. According to *The Chambers Dictionary* (new edition, 1993), it means 'a division of a pre-industrial nation or people for political purposes, a set of people theoretically of common descent, an aggregate of families, forming a community, a race, a breed, a class or set of people' (p. 1849). The *Cambridge International Dictionary of English* (1995, p. 1556) defines it as 'a group of people, often of related families, who live together, sharing the same language, culture and history, esp. those who do not live in towns or cities and do not have industry or writing. A tribe can also be a large family or other group you belong to.' The *Dictionary of Anthropology* defines tribes as 'a social group usually with a definite area, dialect, cultural homogeneity and unchanging social organisation. It may include several sub-groups such as villas or villages. A tribe ordinarily has a leader and may have a common ancestor as well as a patron deity. The families are small communities making up the tribes linked through economic, social, religious, family or blood tie.'[46] The *Encylopaedia Britannica* cites the definition given by W.H.R. Rivers according to whom it is 'a social group of a simple kind, the members of which speak a common dialect, have a single government, and act together for such common purposes as warfare.' By way of explanation it is added that it is necessary to understand by a single government a political unity of a very simple kind, which may not imply the existence of any obvious mechanism of government, such as hereditary monarchy or an elected council with which we are familiar amongst the civilised people.[47] It will be seen that despite some vital differences in the different definitions, the common points are subscription by a commonness of religious beliefs and practices, language, social structure, all of a primitive nature, and area. And all these criteria are applicable in a general way to the tribal groups in North-Eastern India as to most others elsewhere on the earth, though certain groups like the Bodos are characterised also by difference of dialects and religious beliefs and practices.

We feel, however, that the origin of tribes can be better hypothesised on the basis of the concept of areas of attraction and isolation coupled with the inertia of the people concerned. The areas gifted with fertile soil and other means of easy living and easy accessibility from and to other areas providing opportunities of contact with the outside world were sure to promote greater cultural development than other areas not so well-provided for by nature and insulated by insurmountable mountain barriers. Of course, a small group of enterprising people would, even under highly adverse circumstances, make a world of difference no matter what the barriers are. Similarly, even under very favourable physical conditions a lethargic group is liable to remain backward. If man had allowed himself to be governed by only physical conditions, all the communities in a similar situation would have had a similar level of development which, as we know, is not the case. And man would have not attained the state of civilisation that he has. Moreover, the criterion of backwardness is not always the same. Some human groups may be materially not that well off, but on the plane of philosophical and religious thought may have gone very high. And some of the tribal groups of the North-East have a highly intricate philosophical thought matching with the loftiest ones.[48] As such it is perhaps not proper to treat all the so-called tribes as backward and primitive. In fact, it is a great injustice to them.

The natural influx of people and ideas as well as cultural elements from the rest of India beyond its western borders has been commonly described by both Occidental and Indian savants hitherto as an attempt at Āryanisation or Sanskritisation, Sanskrit language and culture represented by it being treated as an inseparable concomitant of the so-called Āryan culture. These ideas have been repeated even as late as 1993[49] by as enlightened a scholar as N.N. Bhattacharyya in his lectures in this very series though he has evinced a much greater awareness of the cultural development of these tribal groups of the North-East. In all these attempts the word *ārya* has been treated as one endowed with a racial or linguistic connotation, and the idea has been that of an imposition of an alien culture over racially different peoples as in the case of a religion together with its concomitants intruding forcibly with the outside invaders like the various shades of Europeans in modern times who brought and tried to impose Christianity on these people with ostensible patronage, support and encouragement of the ruling classes. The fact, however, is that in ancient India the word was never employed in a racial or linguistic sense as would be obvious to any impartial observer who cares to peruse early Indian literary or epigraphic records. The votaries of all the indigenous Indian religions like Vedicism, Paurāṇicism, Buddhism, Jainism and all other sects used it to express their high regards for a respectable individual or something otherwise deserving of esteem. Thus the term is found employed for the saints, scholars and noble ideas and practices like the Buddha's four truths (*ārya-satyas*) and eightfold path (*ārya-*

ashṭāṅga-mārga). The Jaina tradition describes twenty-five and a half countries as Ārya-deśas because they were made worth living for the Jaina ascetics and as the Tathāgatas, Baladevas and Vāsudevas[50] were born there.[51] The *Amara-kośa* (not later than fifth century AD) takes *ārya* as synonymous with *kulīna* (high-born) along with similar other words denoting high birth and gentleness.[52] According to a popular definition, an *ārya* is one 'who observes his prescribed duties and refrains from what should not be done and is steadfast in his duties.'[53] Pāṇini (sixth century BC) appears to have employed *ārya* in a technical sense: when coupled with the words *brāhmaṇa* and *kumāra, ārya* denotes the prime minister and the crown prince respectively, while in the expressions like *ārya-kṛita* and *ārya-kṛitī* it denoted a free person.[54] It is obviously used in the latter sense in the *Arthaśāstra* of Kauṭilya (late fourth century BC) in its section dealing with slaves and servants (III. 13) which speaks of the members of all the four traditional *varṇa*-groups as *ārya* (III. 13. 1) and avers that an *ārya* cannot be enslaved (III.13. 4) and that those offering themselves for slavery for some inescapable reasons were liable to be freed on payment of compensation (*mūlya,* III. 13. 15), and that even a person captured under the banner ought to be liberated by suitable work for a specified period or for half the price (III. 13. 19).[55] Similarly, the modes of address like *ārya*, *ārye* and *ārya-putra* for revered personages frequently met with in classical Sanskrit and Prakrit literature[56] would be quite ridiculous and inexplicable if one were to take the word in question in a racial sense. In short, in all these and other cases the word has to be understood as meaning 'noble', 'Sir' and 'Madam', and not as belonging to the so-called Ārya racial or linguistic group. In fact, the word *ārya* had originally a technical sense of 'ploughman' or 'agriculturist' with its origin lying in the root *ȧr*, 'to plough' or 'cultivate'[57] or in the word *irā* meaning 'earth'.[58] Naturally, the derivative of these words, *arya* came to denote a member of the vaiśya class as he owned the land and busied himself with economic activities, the most prominent one being cultivation or agriculture and land being the most valuable possession. Another derivative, *ārya* with accent in the first letter (*ādy-udātta*) came to denote a cultured person, for initially the wealthy were also supposed to be cultured.

The word *ārya* was given a racial sense only in recent centuries by the Occidental scholars, mostly with the vested interest of providing a much-needed academic support to the political ambitions of their patrons. The European invaders of India found in it a double-edged weapon and used it in two ways: first, trying to bring the conquered Indians close to them by telling that they both (invading Europeans and North Indians) hailed from the same racial stock and that the latter had separated from the original stock and land much earlier[59] and had in consequence become lethargic and contaminated by contact with the original inhabitants of India[60] and that they themselves followed them later and therefore were more energetic and less contaminated; on the other hand, they tried to divide the Indians by telling them that North Indians were Āryans and were not original inhabitants of India coming as they did in a hoary past from outside and were different racially from other Indians who had either immigrated to India from some other land before the Āryans or originally belonged to India. It thus helped them rule over the Indians without much resistance by resorting to the well-known strategy of divide and rule. We already know how the Ārya race and a Germanic original home theory came so very handy in the twentieth century to Hitler in the pursuit of his hegemonic aspirations and how it divided Indians vertically.[61]

The discovery of the Harappan culture[62] in the twenties of the twentieth century also came handy to them. The culture as noticed at Harappa and Mohenjo-daro was in a mature or fully developed form without any indication of its antecedent evolution and decline. It was thus supposed to have an abrupt beginning and end, the latter dated by Mortimer Wheeler around 1500 BC. And the destruction of this civilisation was attributed to the sudden Āryan invasion from the West. It was argued that the Āryan invaders rode the horse which was unknown to the Harappans and were as a result able to move swiftly and destroy their foes rather easily, and that the urban civilisation of the Harappans gave way to rural culture of the Vedic age. It was asserted that the Vedic literature shows no awareness of urban life, script, idol-worship, maritime trade, etc., which were the hallmarks of the Harappan culture. But now it is well established as a result of subsequent fieldwork and dispassionate analytical study of the vast Vedic literature that all these presumptions are totally unfounded. The discovery of an unimaginably large number of Harappan sites in post-partition India has shown the untenability of the notion that it flourished only in the Indus valley, and it is now well-known that the hub of the civilisation lay in the basin of the now mostly dried up Sarasvatī river and its tributaries in Indo-Pakistan subcontinent and even the earlier nomenclature (Indus civilisation) has been rendered inadequate to indicate the area of its prevalence. And several sites have given evidence of its beginnings and decline, so that it is now established that its beginning and end lay in the subcontinent itself and that in search of its origins we need not go anywhere else and that the end was not an abrupt event but there was a gradual decline due to natural and man-made causes and imbalances. Then, undeniable evidence of the presence of domesticated horse has also been found from several sites, and it has also been shown that the *Ṛigveda*, not to speak of the other Vedic Saṁhitas, contains enough evidence of the flourishing urban life together with prosperous trade, both inland and seaborne, industrial growth and mineral exploitation, script and language, and image-worship. It has also been shown that several scenes depicted on the Harappan seals and sealings can be explained with the help of Ṛigvedic descriptions. Moreover, the inhabitants of the Harappan centres were physically very similar to the modern inhabitants of the surrounding areas. To sum up, all the bases of the sudden emergence and a violent destruction of the Harappan culture have lost all meaning.[63]

In fine then, all the premises of the Āryan race and invasion theory stand demolished. And consequently it is in the interest of an unbiased historical appreciation of developments in the North-East to put a full stop to thinking in terms of an Āryanisation or Sanskritisation as done by all the historians hitherto. In fact, the Europeans were responsible for it to a great extent. The British in order to perpetuate their rule tried to project the idea of this region being isolated and impenetrable due mainly to its apparent physical diversities in the form of highly elevated mountainous areas and riparian tracts, forested and marshy regions, and kept it to themselves by regulating through government orders entry of outsiders in these areas. Actually, these measures made the region quite inaccessible to others. In this motivated effort they were helped materially by the Christian missionaries who tried to further this imposed isolation by converting the so-called tribal people to Christianity which cut them off not only from their earlier life-style but also from their beliefs and practices which hereafter became only an anathema and a matter of just an academic curiosity. It was quite different from the earlier so-called Hinduisation which was assimilative in nature and accepted, not converted, them together with their religious faith and accorded their divinities a respected status by linking them with their own mythology and principal deities and accepted their socio-religious practices as local customs (*deśāchāra* or *lokāchāra*) which were to be adhered to by the new entrants. Thus, there was a fundamentally qualitative difference between their entry into the religions under the purview of Hinduism and their becoming Christian: the former assimilated them and their socio-religious persuasions as they were and refrained from snapping their link with their past, while the latter adopted the policy of converting them to an entirely different religion and made the new converts completely strangers to their life-style and system of beliefs.[64]

3. EARLY CONTACTS

We shall in these pages attempt to trace the links, political and cultural, between this region and the rest of India during the ancient period. The treatment of the subject is bound to be somewhat sketchy in the absence of adequate dependable data as well as obvious restraints of space. But it will be seen that what is extant is enough to indicate that they were inseparably linked politically and culturally from the earliest known historical period.

The Vedic Period

Some scholars have tried to prove that the Vedic literature shows awareness of Prāgjyotisha or Kāmarūpa as distinct spatial areas. Importance from this point of view has been attached to the Videgha-Māthava episode narrated in the *Śatapatha-brāhmaṇa* (IV. I. 17) which is supposed to indicate an early attempt at the Āryanisation of the Āssām region. The story goes that king Videgha Māthava of the Sarasvatī region held Agni or fire in his mouth. On his uttering a *mantra* the fire leaped down and proceeded eastwards, dried up all the rivers until it reached the Sadānīrā which it left unburnt. As it was not touched by Agni, it was believed to be impure with no brāhmaṇa coming from the west ever crossing it. But it instructed king Videgha Māthava to settle down to the east of this river, and the land was purified with the observance of sacrifices by the brāhmaṇas who crossed it and settled beyond it. This gave the region to the east of the Sadānīrā the name Videha as well as Māthava. The Sadānīrā is said to have formed the dividing line between Kosala and Videha. Now, Sāyaṇāchārya in his commentary cites a *nighaṇṭu* (lexicon) passage treating the rivers Sadānīrā and Karatoyā as identical.[65] And, as the mediaeval *Tāntric* texts like the *Kālikā-purāṇa*[66] and the *Yoginī-tantra*[67] speak of the Karatoyā as forming the western boundary of Kāmarūpa, V.R.R. Dikshitar [68] and, following him, some other scholars[69] regard Sadānīrā (Karatoyā) as the western boundary of Kāmarūpa during the age of the composition of the *Śatapatha-brāhmaṇa*. But since the *Brāhmaṇa* itself avers that the Sadānīrā was the boundary between Kosala and Videha and it is reiterated by Sāyaṇa as well,[70] the theory falls flat.[71]

J.C. Ghosh, [72] followed by some other historians,[73] is of the opinion that a passage of the *Sāṅkhyāyana-gṛhyasūtra*[74] contains a reference to Prāgjyotisha. Although there is no doubt that the word *prāgjyotisha* does occur in the passage under review, it is there employed clearly in the sense of 'before the appearance of light' as shown by the context. The passage dilates upon the rites to be observed in connection with a vow known as Śākka-vrata and enjoins that its performer who is a brahmachārin (student) along with his teacher should first set out in the dusk towards the northern quarter and on seeing some inauspicious objects in that direction should return to their abode. Next it is stated that they should once again proceed to some sacred region prior to the appearance of light and perform further rites like circumambulation before sunrise. As the entire act of going and observing the rituals is to be completed prior to the sunrise, it is apparent that any reference to the Prāgjyotisha is just an impossibility.[75]

The same is true of the alleged allusions to Kāmarūpa or Prāgjyotisha in the *Aitareya* or *Gopatha Brāhmaṇas*.[76]

Thus, the Vedic literature contains no reference to Assam or any other region of the North-East. But the absence of reference need not of necessity be taken to indicate the lack of knowledge of this region on the part of the composers of the vast Vedic literature. Had they been aware that their writings would be harnessed in future as a source-book of history and non-reference construed as an indication of their ignorance of the things concerned, they would have mentioned each and every thing known to them, which was certainly not their objective. But that they were most probably aware of this region and its inhabitants may most probably be inferred from the mention of the Kirāta people in the *Vājasaneyī Saṁhitā* of the *Yajurveda* (XXX. 16), the *Atharva-veda* (X. 4. 14) and the *Taittirīya-brāhmaṇa* (III. 4. 12. 1), for the people of this area are spoken of commonly as Kirāta in early Indian literature as will be seen in the sequel.

PĀṆINI'S *ASHṬĀDHYĀYĪ*

The celebrated Sanskrit grammarian Pāṇini, who either preceded the Buddha or was his near contemporary,[77] shows awareness of this region. His *Ashṭādhyāyī* (IV. 1. 170)[78] speaks of Sūramasa as one of the *janapadas* of the east (*Prāchya-janapada*), the others being Kosala, Kāśi, Magadha and Kaliṅga.[79] And it is further interesting to note that it was a monarchy under a kshatriya king. The name apparently refers to the Surma valley of Assam and its northern hilly region now forming part of Bangladesh. This reference is of immense value for the history of the region under consideration inasmuch as it reveals that the Surma valley had a separate political existence and a monarchical constitution. It should suffice to indicate that around sixth-fifth century B.C, when the grammatical text was composed, the North Indians[80] were well acquainted with the rivers and the hilly regions in the interior of this area.[81]

EARLY BUDDHIST CANONICAL LITERATURE

Pali literature datable to early period contains no definite reference to the North-Eastern region, and we have also no mention of Prāgjyotisha or Kāmarūpa which most probably indicates that Buddhism had not yet made headway in this region. But it was definitely aware of the prevalence and popularity of Vedic religion and culture in the region of the Brahmaputra as will follow from references to the episode of a Lohichcho brāhmaṇa in the Buddhist Pali canonical works *Dīgha-nikāya*[82] and *Saṁyutta-nikāya.*[83] Lohichcha is evidently a Prakrit form of the Sanskṛit name Lauhitya (Brahmaputra) which itself, according to some, may have been Sanskritised from 'the Indo-Mongoloid (Old Boḍo ?) name *Luhit* which is still the name of the easternmost branch of the river, now flanked by Mishmi (North Assamese), Singpho or Kachin (Burmese Kuki-Lolo) and Khamati (Siamese-Chinese speakers)'.[84] But it is more likely that Luhit was a local colloquial form of the Sanskrit name Lohita or Lauhitya. The lack of interest of the early Buddhists whose mentality these passages reflect can easily be appreciated from the fact that it was beyond the pale of early Buddhism[85] and had become at the same time a stronghold of Vedic religion and culture. And it need not be taken as an evidence of the absence of knowledge of the region to the east of this river, as will be evident from the afore-cited evidence of Panini's *Ashṭādhyāyī* which was composed considerably earlier.

THE EPICS: *RĀMĀYAṆA* AND *MAHĀBHĀRATA*

While the traditional age of the episodes narrated in the two epics is of a hoary antiquity not countenanced by ascertained history, the date of their composition is much later, and according to modern literary historians none of them in their present form can be dated earlier than 500 BC, while the *terminus a quo* lies much beyond the commencement of the Christian era. According to the generally accepted view, the former text is to be dated between the fourth-third century BC and, with all the additions, end-second century AD,[86] and the latter between the fourth century BC and fourth century AD.[87]

The former text refers to the city of Prāgjyotisha as situated on the Varāha mountain in the midst of an unfathomable sea and as the abode of the demon named Naraka.[88] Unfortunately the value of this specific reference is marred considerably by its confused mention in course of the regions to the west which were to be visited by the monkeys under the leadership of Sushena despatched by Sugrīva in search of Sītā abducted by Rāvaṇa. Evidently the author of these stanzas, whosoever he was, had no idea at all of its location and was just eager to refer to it as it had already become a celebrated town. But there is no doubt whatsoever about it being the homonymous capital of the country of the same name in view of its association with the Varāha mountain and the demon Naraka which are closely connected with the North-East and all the later ruling families of Kāmarūpa or Prāgjyotisha trace their origin from or speak of their association with them. But at the same time we need not attach undue importance to the description of its being situated on the Varāha mountain which itself is said to have been located in the midst of (or on) the ocean.[89]

But the *Mahābhārata* shows much more dependable acquaintance with the country and city of Prāgjyotisha and contains several references scattered all over the text, particularly because it was traditionally believed to have played a significant role in the Mahābhārata episode. It refers not just to Prāgjyotisha but also to Naraka and his birth from god Vishṇu in his Varāha (Boar) manifestation and the earth, his being killed by Kṛishṇa and to his son and successor Bhagadatta who are repeatedly mentioned in Assamese chronicles as well as copperplate charters in connection with the origin and early history of the local dynasties.[90]

As to **Naraka**, we find from Uddyotaparvan that he was associated with the city and fort of Prāgjyotisha and styled *Bhauma* ('son of Bhūmi', viz. earth) and said to have stolen the bejewelled earrings of the divine mother Aditi. The gods led by Śakra could not defeat him in war because of Vishṇu's weapon (*Vaishṇavāstra*) received by him from god Vishṇu and at their entreaty Kṛishṇa killed him together with his retinue.[91] In the same Parvan at another place we are told that Kṛishṇa killed Naraka, who had lived for several aeons, at Nirmochana near Prāgjyotisha and rescued thousands of girls from his control whom later he wedded.[92] At another place he is called 'son of earth' (*jagatyās tanaya*).[93] At yet another place his killing by god Vishṇu, his bones looking like a mountain and Vishṇu's act of rescuing the earth in his Varāha (Boar) form and the *kshobha* (commotion) resulting from this act are described[94] in such a manner as to approximate the tradition of Naraka's birth from this act, though it is not stated explicitly.

We get many more references to **Bhagadatta** mainly because of and in connection with his participation in the Bhārata war which have a much more historical look as compared to those about Naraka. Kṛishṇa in the Droṇaparvan (XXIX. 1-36) is reported to have told Arjuna how Vishṇu gave Naraka his weapon and how it came to Prāgjyotisha and Bhagadatta who is described as a Prāgjyotisha king. He was closely associated with the Mahābhārata heroes and the Bhārata war and naturally claims much attention. In the Ādiparvan (LXVII. 9) he is mentioned as an Asura together with Bāshkala.[95] He participated in Draupadī's *svayaṁvara* together with other kings (Ādi, CLXXXV. 12). Though an ally of Jarāsandha, he was Pāṇḍu's friend and loved Yudhishṭhira like his own son (Sabhā, XIV. 14-16). In the context of the *digvijaya* (conquest of quarters) attendant on Yudhishṭhira's Rājasūya sacrifice he, aided by an army comprising primarily of Chīna and Kirīta soldiers as well as those living on the ocean and marshy regions (*sīgar-ānīpa-vīsibhiḥ*), had to fight a sanguine war lasting for full eight days with Arjuna in course of the latter's northern expedition, but being impressed by his valour agreed to conduct himself according to his wishes and to pay taxes to Yudhishṭhira. It was due also to his being friendly with Indra and Pāṇḍu (Sabhā, XXVI. 7-16). We are also told that Bhīma during his eastern campaign reached the Lauhitya region and forced all the Mlechchha kings to pay taxes and present jewels, sandalwood, aloe wood, clothes, pearls, precious stones, blankets, gold, silver and coral in quantities (*ibid.*, XXX. 26-29). Bhagadatta, though not named in this context, may have been the most prominent of the kings as would follow from the mention of the Lauhitya which bordered his kingdom on the west. It may as well indicate that the Prāgjyotisha king was not included among the Mlechchha monarchs reportedly humbled by Bhīma. He is described as the lord of Prāgjyotisha (*Prāgjyotish-ādhipa*) and the Mlechchhas (*Mlechchhānām = adhipa)* and represented as accompanied by the Yavanas at the court of Yudhishṭhira on the occasion of his Rājasūya with presents including fast-moving horses of excellent breed, swords with pure ivory handles and ornaments studded with precious stones (*ibid.*, LI. 14-16). Karṇa is also said to have won a victory over him and thereafter marched to the Himavat mountain and Nepal (Vana, CCLIV. 5-7).[96] Drupada suggested inviting him to fight on the side of the Pāṇḍavas, and, what is interesting in this connection, he is mentioned as inhabiting (the region of) the eastern ocean (*pūrva-sāgara-vāsin*, Uddyoga, IV. 11). We are not told if the invitation was actually sent, but he, accompanied by his army comprising the Chīnas and the Kirātas, went to fight in aid of Duryodhana (*ibid.*, XIX. 15). He fought in the war right from the opening day with several heroes including Virāṭ (Bhīshma, XLV. 49-51), Ghaṭotkacha (*ibid.*, LXIV. 59-62; LXXXIII. 32-38), Sātyaki (*ibid.*, CXI. 7-13), Bhīmasena (*ibid.*, LXIV. 47-54; XCV. 76; CXIII-CXIV), the Daśārṇa king (*ibid.*, XCV. 46-49, Droṇa, XXVI. 37-39), Kshatradeva (*ibid.*, XCV. 73), Drupada (*ibid.*, XIV. 40-42) and Ruchiparvan (*ibid.*, XXVI. 52-53) with varying results, and finally with Arjuna at whose hands he died (Bhīshma, CXIII-CXIV; CXVI. 56-60; Droṇa, XIV-XXIX). Bhagadatta was succeeded after his death in the Bhārata war by his son Vajradatta who, too, had to taste a defeat at the hands of Arjuna finding an opportunity to avenge his father's death (Āśvamedhika, LXXVI. 1-26).

From these accounts of Bhagadatta two things stand out prominently. These concern the nature of the population of his kingdom and the extent of Prāgjyotisha.

First, his army and apparently the subjects included the Chīnas and the Kirātas which would show the mixed character of the population of the North-East where he ruled. And secondly, during his reign Prāgjyotisha was very extensive, and the inclusion of the area from the Bay of Bengal in the south to the Himalayan mountains in the north is most probably suggested by the employment of the descriptive epithets *Pūrva-sāgara-vāsin* and *Parvata-pati* for him at several places as we have just seen. Almost the whole area presently covered by the states newly carved out of Assam appears to have formed the sphere of its influence, if not, conceptually at least, its integral part.

Another important fall-out of the descriptions of wars wherein Bhagadatta is reported to have been involved is the highly significant role played by the elephants. The excellent qualities of his elephant called Supratīka are highlighted as well as Bhagadatta's heroic deeds are detailed (Bhīshma, LIX, and Droṇa, XXVI. 4) in connection with his fatal war with Arjuna. He is eulogised as 'not inferior to Indra in battle and expert in driving elephants'. Even his dreaded enemy Arjuna, who would hardly be expected to indulge in hyperbolics about him, is high praise for his elephant forces (*ibid.*, XXVI. 5ff.). It is thus clear that elephantry had a highly important place in the forces of Bhagadatta, and this leads us to the inference that as at present elephants were available in profusion in ancient Kāmarūpa also.

As we have seen, Vajradatta, who fought Arjuna valiantly in course of the latter's campaign of protecting the sacrificial horse, was son and successor of Bhagadatta. Another son of Bhagadatta was Kṛitaprajña who is said to have been killed by Nakula in the Bhārata war (Karṇa, V. 28).[97]

The legend about the demon king Bāṇa also figures in the *Mahābhārata*. In its southern recension we are told that his capital was at Śoṇitapura[98] which has generally been equated by historians with modern Tezpur in Assam.[99] He was a great devotee of Śiva whose favour he enjoyed. Kṛishṇa's son Aniruddha is said to have fallen in love with his daughter and was imprisoned by Bāṇa and in the battle that ensued Kṛishṇa killed Bāṇa by his Sudarsana wheel.[100]

What is particularly noticeable in the present context is that while the name Prāgjyotisha is encountered repeatedly in various contexts, we do not come across the other name Kāmarūpa, which had come into existence by the first century BC as indicated by Kālidāsa's above-cited allusions, even once in either of the epics. This should suffice to establish that these portions belong to their earlier stratum which must have been composed considerably prior to their suggested *terminus a quo*.[101]

Thus the *Mahābhārata* links Bhagadatta and Vajradatta and the latter's brother Kṛitaprajña closely with the Bhārata war. And in view of the fact that these traditions attained such a great currency during the later centuries and are found mentioned off and on in later literary and inscriptional sources, it is not unlikely that the episodes have some historical substratum though they are naturally magnified beyond proportions and need not be taken at their face value.[102]

Now, the historians are generally agreed that the Bhārata war was a historical event though fought on a much smaller scale between two factions of a very powerful ruling line with several other ruling families fighting on one or other side. However, there is a wide divergence on the question of its date, both in ancient traditions and among modern historians. The most widely popular tradition dates it in 3102 BC as related by the celebrated astronomer Āryabhaṭa[103] and repeated by poet Ravikīrti in the Aihoḷe inscription (dated AD 634) of the early Chalukya emperor Pulakeśin II.[104] But there were also traditions which placed this event some centuries later. According to a very persistent convention, it took place in 2449 (current) or 2448 (expired) BC. This notion is first referred to by Varāhamihira who in his *Bṛihatsaṁhitā* (XIII. 3) gives the interval between the period of the Mahābhārata hero Yudhishṭhira and the commencement of the Śaka era as 2526 years.[105] Some modern Indian astronomers have tried to demonstrate that even some astronomical references in the *Mahābhārata* itself support this date.[106] The Kashmiri chronicler Kalhaṇa in his *Rāja-taraṅgiṇī* (I. 56) cites the above statement of Varāhamihira, dubs the notion that the Bhārata war occurred at the end of Dvāpara as misleading (I.49) and asserts that the Kurus and the Pāṇḍavas lived after 653 years of the Kali age had elapsed.[107] This tradition is also sought to be buttressed on the strength of a certain assertion in one of the charters of the Prāgjyotisha monarch Bhāskaravarman. It is averred in his Nidhānpur Plates (verse 7) that Vajradatta, son of Bhagadatta, who had participated in the Bhārata war, was followed by his descendants who ruled for three thousand years after which Pushyavarman became king.[108] And as Bhāskaravarman, who was a contemporary of Harshavardhana of Sthāṇvīśvara and Kannauj and flourished around in the first half of the seventh century AD, was twelfth in descent (and thirteenth ruler) from Pushyavarman, the latter may be placed in the second quarter of the fourth century AD. And adding to it 3000 years reportedly elapsed between him and Bhagadatta's son Vajradatta, we reach about 2450 BC, tallying well with 2449-2448 BC.[109] There is yet another tradition based on the varying statements in the Purāṇas about the interval between Parīkshit, grandson of Arjuna and successor of Yudhishṭhira, and the coronation of Mahāpadma (Nanda) who flourished latest in the fourth century BC prior to the accession of Chandragupta Maurya. It is given as 1050 or 1015 years, and accordingly the Bhārata war may be dated in around fifteenth century BC. But after a careful comparison of the Paurāṇic passages on this question and the duration of time allotted to various dynasties, P.V. Kane has concluded that the correct reading most probably was *pañcha-śat-ottaram*, and not *pañchāśaduttaram* or *pañchadaś-ottaram* as found in the printed editions of the Purāṇas concerned. And consequently the gap between Parīkshit and Mahāpadma Nanda's coronation ought to be 1500, not 1015 or 1050, years and therefore, following this tradition, the Bhārata war will have to be placed around 1900 BC.[1110] However, archaeologists, who concede the historicity of the war, are not prepared to concede any of these traditional dates and are inclined to date it somewhere between 900 and 1400 BC basing on the time-bracket for the Painted Grey Ware (PGW) culture noticed at most of the sites in northern India traditionally associated with the activities of the Kauravas and the Pāṇḍavas and the Bhārata war and some other considerations.[111] The find of some other material including a few seals in the underwater excavations at Beṭ Dwārakā in layers dating from around fifteenth century BC has been taken by the excavator[112] to confirm Kṛishṇa's association with the site during this period.

Thus, the epics, especially the *Mahābhārata*, provide the bases, in a germinal form in some cases, of the legends which are found highly developed in later Sanskrit Purāṇic and Tāntric texts as well as inscriptions. Of Naraka, for example, we have the following details more or less developed: he was born of the earth, had close relation with the Varāha manifestation of god Vishṇu, was lord of the city and kingdom of Prāgjyotisha, obtained an infallible weapon from Vishṇu (*Vaishṇavāstra*) and carried away the earrings of the divine mother Aditi, at the entreaty of divinities Kṛishṇa defeated and killed him with his retinue and recovered Aditi's earrings and took for his wives thousands of women captured by him. Regarding Naraka's son Bhagadatta, we are told that he succeeded Naraka on the throne of Prāgjyotisha, received Vishṇu's weapon from Kṛishṇa who restored it to him at the earth's request, his participation in the Bhārata war on the side of the Kauravas and being killed at the hands of Arjuna and being succeeded on the throne by his son Vajradatta. On this foundation the *Purāṇakāras* and the composers of later inscriptions of Kāmarūpa built up the fully developed historico-mythical superstructure met with in their compositions. Various facets of this legend are met with in a fully developed form in the *Harivaṁśa*, *Vishṇu, Bhāgavata-*, *Brahmā* and *Agni-purāṇas,* while the *Kālikā-purāṇa* and the *Yoginī-tantra,* which were composed in Kāmarūpa during early mediaeval period, give the whole legend as current in the region at the time of their composition.[113]

The copperplate charters dating from the time of Bhāskaravarman, who lived in the first half of the seventh century AD and played a significant role in pan-Indian politics like his traditional ancestor Bhagadatta and brought the North-East on the national politico-cultural map of India, trace the origin of the family from the earth and god Vishṇu's Varāha (Boar) manifestation and from Bhagadatta whom they describe as Naraka's son and successor. It is further averred that Bhagadatta participated in the Bhārata war and lost his life only to be succeeded on the throne by Vajradatta who was his son according to most of the sources and brother according to some later charters.[114] As we have just seen, we also come across a statement in the Nidhānpur charter of Bhāskaravarman that has an important bearing on the problem of the date of the Bhārata war since when the family reportedly to have begun its rule.

Despite the persistence of these traditions, however, it is difficult, nay impossible, to believe that a family ruling over so far off a region, as Prāgjyotisha undoubtedly was, participated in a rather small, albeit very important and epoch-making, war between the two groups of the same family as Bhārata war indubitably was. Physical distances were too great, especially in such an early age when means of communication were undoubtedly not that fast, to permit it. Some historians therefore appear to be not far off the point when they doubt the historicity of these traditions and hold that 'Bhagadatta's association with the Bhārata war and the Kuru-Pāṇḍavas is a later invention' and that 'he did not actually fight in the war'. They may also be right in assuming that Naraka was a dynastic name.[115] But then how to account for the persistent traditions ?

Actually the *Mahābhārata* is not a unified work by a single author or belonging to one period and underwent the process of constant additions and alterations from time to time. An express statement contained in the extant work itself admits of its passing through no less than three stages of growth which must have covered quite a few centuries. The original work comprising just 8,800 stanzas is reported to have been composed by Kṛishṇa Dvaipāyana Vyāsa and was known as Jaya as it concerned itself simply with the central event, viz. the victory (*jaya*) of the Pāṇḍavas over the Kauravas in the factional war between them. It was subsequently revised and enlarged by Vaiśampāyana (and probably his school) with the accretion of fresh material. It now turned into *Bhārata* consisting of 24,000 verses. And finally with the addition of many a dose of fresh matter with the object of turning the work into something like an encyclopaedia of Indian culture with all its components[116] it assumed the form of a virtual compendium of all the then existing knowledge captioned *Mahābhārata* with 100,000 stanzas called appropriately *śata-sāhasrī saṁhitā*.

Obviously the entire episode centring round Naraka and Bhagadatta was concocted in later times with the motive of securing a high antiquity and resultant legitimacy for the rule of the most prominent local ruling family and was later inherited by other lines. Another object of tracing the origin from god Vishṇu (in his boar manifestation) and the goddess earth may have been to impart it a hallowed lineage, and the Naraka episode may have been intended to satisfy the aspirations of the mixed local populace. And the priestly class must have undoubtedly played a pivotal role in the entire development. Such practices, it is pertinent to remember, were not confined to Prāgjyotisha alone; they are, in fact, found in almost all the regions of Bhāratavarsha.

If so, when was the legend invented and attained widespread popularity ? As we have just seen, the *Mahābhārata* mentions only the older name Prāgjyotisha whereas the other name, viz. Kāmarūpa, which appears to have come into being by the first century BC, is conspicuous by its absence. We would therefore not be far wrong in concluding that the whole of Bhagadatta legend had already attained popularity prior to this date.

There perhaps may have been some rationale behind the whole thing and it might not have been entirely baseless. A possible reason for the invention might have been the similarity of some of the names. It is not impossible that Pṛithivī and Varāha were human personages who begot a son named Naraka. And as these were also the names of divinities (in the first two cases) and of demons (in the last case) the myths concerning them got applied to them in consequence of which they were turned into mythical figures. Once they are shorn of these myths, they turn into historical beings. Because of his wicked deeds or so construed by his detractors, Naraka was defeated and killed by the invaders and, as usually happens in such cases, his son Bhagadatta was placed on the vacant throne by a person named Kṛishṇa as his protégé. As will be seen in the next chapter, Naraka was a historical personage, being the father of the first known historical monarch, Pushyavarman, and this might have been projected in the hoary past.

THE MAURYA AGE

It is doubtful if the North-Eastern region formed part of or was in any way connected politically with the Maurya empire. That it was outside the Maurya, particularly Aśokan, empire is probably indicated by the absence of any reference to any of its parts or towns in the edicts of Aśoka as well as the non-availability of any of his inscriptions.[117] The same is indicated by the non-mention of any of the Aśokan monuments by the Chinese pilgrim Yuan Chwang who visited Kāmarūpa about mid-seventh century AD and was anxious to mention them if there existed any. So we may conclude, tentatively at least, that it did not form part of the Maurya empire even during Aśoka's reign.

However, that the region was in close contact with and well-known to the North Indians during the period is clearly attested by the *Arthaśāstra* of Kauṭilya, the prime minister of Chandragupta, the founder of the Maurya empire.

While describing the precious objects to be entered in the royal exchequer (*kośa-praveśya-ratna-parīkshā*),[118] the work refers to certain objects which were produced in the region on the other side of the river Lauhitya (*pāra-Lauhitya*) and some other localities situated in Kāmarūpa. Thus, we are told that the aloe from Joṅgaka was black, black-variegated or variegated with round spots, while that from Doṅga was dark.[119] Incense (*tailaparṇika*) from Aśokagrāma had the colour of flesh and the fragrance of lotus, and that from Joṅga was reddish yellow and was endowed with the fragrance of a blue lotus or smell of bovine urine, while that from Grāmeru was smooth and had the smell of the urine of cow, and that from Suvarṇakuḍya was reddish yellow and had the smell of the citron fruit, and that from Pūrṇaka-dvīpa had the fragrance of a lotus or the smell of butter.[120] The *bhadraśriya*[121] from beyond the Lauhitya had the colour of the *jāti* flower, and that hailing from Antaravatī was of the colour of *uśīra* (andropogon) and both smelled like the costus.[122] According to Bhaṭṭasvīmin's Pratipada-pañchikā and other commentaries most of these places were situated in Kāmarūpa,[123] and the name Pāra-Lauhitya is transparent enough to need any explanation. And as regards Suvarṇakuḍya, it has been proved convincingly by K.L. Barua that it is now represented by the village of Soṇkuḍihā on the Hajo-Nalbari road, about nine miles from Hajo and five miles from Nalbari in the Kāmrūp district and is also known as Phingua-rajar-garh. He has further shown that most of the products are still a speciality of Assam and that consequently Kauṭilya's description is fairly correct.[124]

We may therefore conclude justifiably that even if Kāmarūpa had no or little political connection with the Maurya empire that edged its western frontiers, the two had close commercial relations and the economic products of the former were highly valued and stored in the Mauryan government treasury. Unfortunately, we have as of now absolutely no knowledge about the commodities that the region (or regions) of the North-East received in exchange.

It is pertinent to note in this connection that there is no mention of any commercial product from any of the regions other than those presently included in the state of Āssām. Historians are likely to infer from it that Kauṭilya had no knowledge of the areas now included in Meghalaya, Arunachal Pradesh, Mizoram and Nagaland which is certainly not impossible; it is questionable though whether *argumentum ex silentio* can be treated as a definitive evidence of ignorance.

NOTES AND REFERENCES

1. English translation by H.S. Jarret, Vol. II, p. 131. The reference is to the 'Rājah of Ashām' and his 'great pomp and state'. Abul Fazl, however, seems to distinguish the province from '*Kāmrūp*, commonly called also *Kāonrup* and *Kāmtā*', which was subject to the chief of the country called *Kuch*. *Vide ibid.*, p. 130. Ashām is said to have bordered Lower Tibet and *Khata*, which was 'also called *Mahāchin* which the vulgar pronounced *Māchin*.' But it is not impossible that the author has employed the two names as synonymous, and this position finds some support from the account of the region by Ami Ahmadn's *Haft Iqlim* cited in the next note.
2. Cited by Mohammad Azhar Ansari in his *Geographical Glimpses of Medieval India*, Vol. II, p. 23. He first describes the country of Kuch as 'located between eastern and northern part of Bengala' and its borders are said to 'touch China'. Its 'other border' was Gorāghāṭ. We read further, 'from the borders of China that is called Asham (Assam) till the region of Kuch'.
3. *JASB*, XLI, p. 55.
4. *Travels in India*, I, p. 16; II, p. 277.
5. *Vide* for these references, K.L. Barua, *SEHA*, pp. 270-71. These references should leave no doubt about the connection between the Ahoms and the regional name Asama (Assamese) or its anglicised version Assam.
6. For a detailed account of the Tai Ahoms in a historical and cultural perspective, see Puspadhar Gogoi, *Tai of North-East India*.
7. But *contra IHQ*, III, p. 421, where B. Bhattacharya has pointed out that the Vajrayāna sect of Buddhism and the Bodhisattvas are called *asama* in the Buddhist text *Sādhanamālā* and therefore the region may have been named Asama after them, for the Kāmarūpa region happened to be a Vajrayāna stronghold.
8. E.A. Gait, *A History of Assam*, pp. 245-46.
9. 'The Name Assam-Ahom', *JASB*, XXII, 1956, pp. 147-53 *Kirāta-jana-kṛiti: The Indo-Mangoloids: Contribution to the Society and Culture of India*, pp. 101-2.
10. B.K. Kakati, *AFD*, pp. 1-3; ed. *Aspects of Early Assamese Literature*, pp. 1-2. *Vide* also *New Indian Antiquary*, I, pp. 1-28. This suggestion is adopted partially by B.K. Barua ('A Note on the Word Assam', *JARS*, II, 1935, pp. 103-4).
11. Baden-Powell, *The Indian Village Community*, p. 135.
12. Cited in B.K. Barua, *CHA*, p. 4.
13. A.G. Grierson, *Linguistic Survey of India*, II, p. 5.
14. This view is cited and partially supported by B.K. Barua in the paper cited in *supra* note 4.
15. This has been surmised from B.K. Barua's *CHA*, p. 1.
16. *Vide* R. Gopalakrishnan, 'Land and People in North-Eastern India: An Introduction', in J.P. Singh and G. Sengupta (eds.), *Archaeology of North-Eastern India*, p. 27.
17. The earliest dependable references to Prāgjyotisha occur in the two epics, viz. the *Rāmāyaṇa* and the *Mahābhārata*. That the Vedic literature contains no allusion to it has been demonstrated by Mukund Madhava Sharma. *Vide* his *IAA*, Introduction, pp. 1-3.

18. 'Ancient Countries in Eastern India', *JASB*, 1897, p. 106.
19. *The Mārkaṇḍeya-purāṇa,* Engl. Tr., p. 328,fn.
20. *Vide*, for instance, K.L. Barua, *EHK,* pp. 2, 5-6, etc.
21. For an elaboration of the exact position, see D.C. Sircar, *Studies in the Geography of Ancient and Medieval India*, 2nd edn., pp. 159-65.
22. For a discussion of the *Bṛihatsaṁhitā* reference, *vide* Ajay Mitra Shastri, *Varāhamihira's India*, I, p. 89.
23. The town is now supposed to be represented by the ruins of Dispur, about two miles east of Guwahati. *Vide* K.L. Barua, *EHK,* pp. 12-13.
24. *Kālikā-Purāṇa*, XXXIX. 126. This is, as we shall just see, sought to be supported on some other grounds by a few other scholars. K.L. Barua renders the name Prāgjyotisha by the 'land of rising sun' .
25. E.A. Gait, *History of Assam*, p. 15. He renders Prāgjyotishapura as 'City of Eastern Astrology'.
26. For these and some other evidences, see D.B. Spooner, 'The Zoroastrian Background of Indian History', *JRAS*, 1915, pp. 433-36. K.L. Barua, *EHK,* p. 13; *SEHA*, pp. 12-13, where some more data about the solar cult in Āssām are supplied. See also B.K. Barua, *CHA*, p. 11; P.C. Choudhury, *HCPA*, p. 29. Choudhury also invites attention to the *Bihu* festival associated with solar cult and fertility rites.
27. B.K. Kakati, *The Mother Goddess Kāmākhyā*, p. 6.
28. R. Nath, *The Background of Assamese Culture,* pp. 4-5.
29. For an instance of such contradictions, *vide* P.C. Choudhury, *op. cit.,* pp. 28-29. It is rather surprising to find Choudhury endorsing the rendering of the name Prāgjyotisha as 'the place of eastern astrology' originally proposed by Gait and in the same breath upholding the theory of its non-Āryan origin.

    However, he has rightly shown the untenability of the theories of R.C. Majumdar (pointing out the existence of the Prāgjyotishas in the north-west and their later migration together with the name to Assam in later times) and K.V. Athavale (tracing the original Prāgjyotisha in Kāṭhiāwāḍ and Bhagadatta's coming over to Assam). See *ibid*., pp. 39-40.

    But these references just indicate that there were people or countries known by this name elsewhere in the countries where they might have gone from the original Prāgjyotisha in the east. This was most probably the case with the countries of this name on the Vetravati or Betwa in Central India (B. C. Law) and in the eastern Panjāb (B.M. Barua).
30. *Vide* D.R. Bhandarkar (Reviser), B. Ch. Chhabra and G. S. Gai (editors), *Inscriptions of the Early Gupta Kings, CII*, III, p. 213, line 22.
31. *Kālidāsa-granthāvalī*, ed. Reva Prasad Dvivedi, pp. 177-78, verses 81-84. These references have misled B.K. Barua into believing that Kālidāsa differentiated between Prāgjyotisha and Kāmarūpa. *Vide* his *CHA*, I, p. 12.
32. Like Prāgjyotisha, there were some other countries named Kāmarūpa in certain other regions. Thus the *Śiva, Vāyu* and *Brahmāṇḍa Purāṇas* show awareness of a country of this name in the Sahya mountain and of the Kāmarūpī *rākshasas* on the Devakūṭa mountain. See B.K. Barua, *CHA*,

pp. 12-13. In our opinion these references have, like those to Prāgjyotisha, to be explained in terms of migrations from the eastern region of this name and prove nothing else.

33. For references, see *CHA*, I, p. 12.
34. For the details of these allusions, see *IAA*, pp. 11-13 and 15-18. M.M. Sharma has also listed references to Prāgjyotisha.
35. नेपालस्य काञ्चनाद्रिं ब्रह्मपुत्रस्य सङ्गमम्।
करतोयां समारभ्य यावद् दिक्करवासिनीम्।।
उत्तरायां कञ्जगिरिः करतोया तु पश्चिमे।
तीर्थश्रेष्ठा दिक्षुनदी पूर्वस्यां गिरिकन्यके।।
दक्षिणे ब्रह्मपुत्रस्य लाक्षायाः सङ्गमावधि।
कामरूप इति ख्यातः सर्वशास्त्रेषु निश्चितः।।
36. त्रिंशद् योजनविस्तीर्णं दीर्घेण शतयोजनम्।
कामरूपं विजानीहि त्रिकोणाकारमूर्त्तमम्।।
ईशाने चैव केदारो वायव्यां गजशासनः।
दक्षिणे सङ्गमे देवि लाक्षाया ब्रह्मरेतसः।।
37. *Origin and Development of Bengali Language*, I, p. 69, *Kirāta-jana-kṛiti:*, *The Indo-Mongoloids: Their Contribution to the History and Culture of India*, p. 89.
38. *Mechh* is regarded by some as the original of the Sanskrit *Mlechchha*. *Vide* S.K. Chatterji, *Kirāta-jana-kṛiti*, p. 97. B.K. Barua (*CHA*, I, p. 6), on the other hand, treats the former as a corruption of the latter. The latter view is clearly preferable.
39. It is averred that the earliest inhabitants of Assam were speakers of the Indo-Chinese language of the Mon-Khmer family which has been characterised by some as the Austric family of languages. See *ibid.*, p. 5.
40. For a detailed summary of views and discussion on the racial elements in Assamese population, see P.C. Choudhury, *HCPA*, pp. 81-114.
41. S.K. Chatterji, *Indo-Aryan and Hindi*, p. 39; *CHA*, pp. 5-6.
42. Even Yuan Chwang in the mid-seventh century AD, when Indo-Chinese intercourse had become very frequent, was aware of the difficulties involved in travelling by the mountainous route.
43. See N.N. Bhattacharya, *Religious Culture of North-Eastern India*, pp. 37ff.
44. They are called Kirāta in the Vedic and Epic literature.
45. It applies only to the original inhabitants and those who have settled in modern times in search of livelihood stand excluded.
46. Published by Peter Ovens Ltd., London, p. 536.
47. 1957 edn., Vol. 22, p. 465.
48. For a discussion of the highly developed religio-philosophical thought of some of the so-called tribal groups, *vide* N.N. Bhattacharyya, *op. cit.*, pp. 1-35.
49. The lectures on the *Religious Culture of North-Eastern India* were delivered in 1993 though they appeared two years later in 1995.
50. According to the Jaina tradition, the Baladevas, Vāsudevas and Tathāgatas

were included among the sixty-three Śalākā-purushas, viz. great beings.

51. *Vide* J.C. Jain, *Life in Ancient India as depicted in the Jain Canon,* p. 250.

52. महाकुलकुलीनार्य्यसभ्यसज्जनसाधव: ।
Amara-kosha, with Bhānujidīkshita's Rāmāśramī commentary, II. 7. 3.

53. कर्तव्यमाचरन् काममकर्तव्यमनाचरन् ।
तिष्ठति प्रकृताचारे स तु आर्य इति स्मृत: ।।

54. Vasudeva Sharan Agrawala, *India as known to Pāṇini,* p. 81.

55. We have used in these pages *The Kauṭilīya Arthaśāstra*, edited by R.P. Kangle.

56. Such expressions are often found used in plays and other works in the form of conversation or otherwise.

57. *Vide* V.S. Pathak, 'Semantics of Ārya: Its Historical Implications', in S.B. Deo and S.V. Kamath (eds.), *The Aryan Problem*, pp. 87-90.

58. F. Max Müller, *Selected Essays on Language, Mythology and Religion*, I, pp. 210 and 212; Bhagwan Singh, *The Vedic Harappans*, pp. 27-30.

59. The western scholars postulated a non-Indian original home for the Āryans.

60. Earlier, Draviḍians were also supposed to have come to India as invaders who dispossessed her original inhabitants of their habitat.

61. For a detailed running survey of these views in a historical perspective, see Devendra Swarup, 'Genesis of the Aryan Race Theory and its Application to Indian History', in Deo and Kamath (eds.), *op. cit.*, pp. 30-39.

62. Earlier archaeologists called this civilisation as Indus Civilisation or Culture, but after the discovery of a much larger number of sites of an identical culture in the valley of the river Sarasvatī and its tributaries, it ought to be rechristened as Sarasvatī-Sindhu Civilisation or Indus-Sarasvatī Civilisation, as proposed by several Indian and Pakistani archaeologists in recent years. See S.P. Gupta, *The Indus-Sarasvatī Civilization: Origins, Problems and Issues*. A much better and non-controversial nomenclature would be Harappan Culture following the general practice of the archaeologists to name a culture after its first provenance.

63. There exists a vast literature on recent discoveries of and work at the Harappan sites as well as a reappraisal of known material in the perspective of these later findings and their relationship with the Vedic literature. But for the most recent consolidated appreciation, see Bhagwan Singh, *The Vedic Harappans*, and S.P. Gupta, *Indus-Sarasvatī Civilization. Vide* also our paper, 'The Indus Civilisation and the So-called Aryans', *Saṁskṛiti-sandhāna*, IV, 1991, pp. 64-70.

64. *Vide* N.N. Bhattacharyya, *op. cit.*, pp. 2-6.

65. तथा च निघण्टु: करतोया सदानीरा बाहुदा शैतवाहिनी।
It is actually *Amara-kośa*, I. 10.

66. बहुरोका नाम नदी करतोया प्रदक्षिणे।
उत्तरस्रत्राविनी चास्ते तत्पूर्व कामरूपकम्।।

67. For citation, see *supra* notes 29-30.

68. 'Aryanisation of East India (Assam)', *IHQ*, XXI, 1945, pp. 29-33.

69. P.C. Choudhury, *HCPA*, p. 9.

70. *Hi yasmād evaṁ Māthavāya agnir ādāt tasmāt te Videha-deśā api Māthavā ity-uchyante.* Cited in *IAA*, Introduction, p. 2.
71. For a discussion on this point, see *ibid.*, Introduction, pp. 1-2.
72. In *JARS*, IV, p. 116.
73. See, for instance, P. C. Choudhury, *HCPA*, p. 10.
74. *Tata ..... saṁvatsare pūrṇe .....prabhāta-velāyāṁ prāg udīchīṁ diśaṁ gachchhata .... āma-māṁsaṁ Chaṇḍālaṁ ...... sarvāṇi cha mṛitaka-rūpāṇi eteshām anyatamaṁ dṛishṭvā nivartate .... tato nishkramya* ***prāg-jyotishaṁ*** *puṇyadeśam upagamya anudita āditye 'añjana-gandhi-surabhim' ity-anena mantreṇa udaka-dhārayā pradakshiṇaṁ pūrva-dvāraṁ maṇḍalaṁ kṛitvā .....kuśān durvāṁ cha kshipati. tataḥ 'añjana-gandham' ity-anena mantreṇa śishy-āchāryau praviśataḥ.* Cited in *IAA*, Introduction, p. 3.
75. For a discussion, see *ibid.*, Introduction, pp. 2-3.
76. According to V.R.R. Dikshitar (*IHQ*, XXI, 1945, pp. 29-33), the statement in the *Aitareya-brāhmaṇa* (I. 3. 7) that the gods made Soma the king in the east and therefore in the eastern quarter it is bought (*prāchyāṁ vai diśi devāḥ somaṁ rājānaṁ akriṇan, tasmāt prāchyāṁ diśi diśi krīyate*) pre-supposes the information that 'by barter and by purchase' the brāhmaṇas, who were already settled in Assam, obtained Soma for sacrificial purposes from the tribes living in the hilly regions of Kāmarūpa. But this is a mere conjecture in the absence of any proper name like Prāgjyotisha or Kāmarūpa, for there were several forested or hilly regions in the east. P.C. Choudhury (*HCPA*, p. 10), who cites this reference approvingly, also observes that 'the *Gopatha Brāhmaṇa* records a tradition of the origin of the name *Kāmarūpa,* indicating an early contact of the Aryan and non-Aryan elements'. But it is due just to some misunderstanding as the text does not allude even distantly to such a tradition. See also *IAA*, Introduction, pp. 1-3, for fuller discussion of the problem of supposed Vedic allusions to Assam and its residents.
77. The exact date of Pāṇini cannot be determined, and suggestions on this point range as widely as from the eighth to the fourth century BC.
78. *Dvyañ-Magadha-Kaliṅga-Sūramasādaṇ.* This *sūtra* is given as 170th of the first *pāda* of the fourth chapter in most of the editions, but some like that of Sankaradeva Pathak's (Gurukula Vṛindāvana, Vikrama Saṁvat 1999) give it as 168th *sūtra.*
79. *Vide* V.S. Agrawala, *India as known to Pāṇini*, pp. 38 and 62.
80. Pāṇini was born at Śālātura in the Uttarāpatha division of Bhāratavarsha, which now forms part of Pakistan.
81. Attention to this important reference has been drawn in connection with the history of North-Eastern India for the first time in these pages.
82. *Dīgha-nikāya,* I, Pali Publication Board, Bihar Government, Nālandā, 1958, pp. 191-98, cited by M. M. Sharma in *IAA*, Introduction, p. 4, fn. 9.
83. *Saṁyutta-nikāya*, III, Pali Publication Board, Bihar Government, Nalandā, 1959, pp. 107-11, cited in *IAA*, Introduction, p. 4, fn. 10. The Lohichcha brāhmaṇa is said to have had several students or *antevāsikas* under him.
84. This has been suggested by S.K. Chatterji in his *Kirāta-jana-kṛiti: The Indo-Mongoloids: Their Contribution to the History and Culture of India*, p. 88, and

thereafter reiterated by several writers on the history of North-Eastern India. But we feel that the reverse view taking Luhit as a local form of the Sanskrit name is also equally, if not much more, likely.

85. The sphere of early Buddhism was restricted to the present states of Bihar and Uttar Pradesh and there too the concentration was in certain areas only.
86. See for a detailed discussion of the problem, M. Winternitz, *A History of Indian Literature*, I, pp. 500-517.
87. *Ibid.*, p. 465.
88. Edited with Tilaka, Śiromaṇi and Bhušhaṇa commentaries by Srinivas Shastri Mudholkar, Kishkindhā-kāṇḍa, XLII. 30-31. The description is highly exaggerated and confused. The Varāha mountain is said to have covered an area of sixty-four *yojanas* and to have had golden peaks and the city is also stated to have been golden.
89. P.N. Bhattacharya (*Kāmarūpa-śāsanāvali*, Introduction, p. 1) quotes a stanza from a Bengali manuscript of the *Rāmāyaṇa* (Ādikāṇḍa, Ch. 36) which is cited by Rajanikanta Chakravarti in his Bengali work *Gauḍer Itihāsa* which credits one Amūrtarajas with the foundation of the city of Prāgjyotisha. But the stanza in question is conspicuous by its absence in the printed editions, and therefore one can not put much store by it. The stanza as given in the aforesaid edition with the Tilaka-Śiromaṇi-Bhūshaṇa commentaries, on the other hand, avers that Amūrtarajas founded Dharmāraṇya.
90. We have used in these pages Gita Press edition of the *Mahābhārata* which gives southern recension as well. For a glance at important references, see *Mahābhārata kī Nāmānukramaṇikā* (Hindi), Gita Press, Gorakhpur, V.S. 2016, under the entries 'Naraka', 'Prāgjyotisha', 'Bhauma', 'Bhagadatta' and 'Vajradatta'. Only the southern recension's p. no. is wrongly printed as 804 whereas the correct no. is 337 (p. 176 under 'Naraka' and elsewhere).
91. Uddyogaparvan, CLVIII. 80-84. *Vide* also the southern recension quoted after Sabhāparvan, XXXVIII. 29, at pp. 337ff. which supplies the same description with additional details.
92. *Ibid.*, CXXX. 44-45.
93. *Ibid.*, XXIX. 32.
94. Vanaparvan, Ch. XLII.
95. In the same stanza the demon Bāshkala is mentioned just before Bhagadatta, but there is nothing absolutely to warrant the suggestion (*Mahābhārata kī Nāmānukramaṇikā*, p. 223, under 'Bhagadatta') that Bhagadatta was born from him, even partially.
96. Surprisingly enough, it is said to have been his first success in his northern expedition and thereafter he is said to have ascended the Himavat mountain and after conquering the Haimavatika ('Himalayan') chiefs he proceeded to Nepal whereafter he descended from the mountain and went to east and vanquished the rulers of Aṅga, Vaṅga, Kaliṅga, Śuṇḍika, Mithilā, Magadha, etc.
97. भगदत्तसुतो राजन् कृत्तप्रज्ञो महाबलः ।
श्येनवच्चरता संख्ये नकुलेन निपातितः ।।
There is no doubt that here Kṛitaprajña is a proper name of one of the sons

of Vajradatta and not an adjective of his son (*vide* for this suggestion, *IAA*, Introduction, p. 8), for that would leave us with only an adjective for his son whose name is missing. Likewise it is difficult to identify him with Pushpadatta mentioned by Bāṇabhaṭṭa in his *Harsha-charita* (VII) in between Bhagadatta and Vajradatta (*ibid.*), for that would involve difference in names. A better way to account for the non-mention of any son of Bhagadatta other than Vajradatta in the epigraphic records would be to assume that the two other sons being younger or dead earlier could not come to power and are consequently ignored in them as elsewhere. It is equally possible that Bāṇabhaṭṭa did not have correct information and his mention of Pushpadatta has to be ignored or that as the latter had no son to succeed him or if there was any he may have predeceased him and both were followed by Vajradatta's line which would justify their non-mention in later inscriptions.

98. Southern recension following Sabhāparvan, XXXVIII. 29, pp. 337ff.

99. In local dialect *tez=śoṇita* 'blood'. Thus, Tezpur Soṇitapura.

100. We have mentioned only the legend encountered in the southern recension as this alone has some bearing on the history of the North-East. We have avoided other references deliberately as they have little to do with this region, and may or may not refer to the same personage.

101. In case Kālidāsa lived in the first century BC and the *Raghuvaṁśa*, which contains this name, was composed during this period, as several scholars following the age-old tradition hold, the date of the portions concerned should lie before this date. For a discussion of these and other references to Prāgjyotisha in the *Mahābhārata*, see our paper in *Mahābhārata: Some Facets* (ed.), Ajay Mitra Shastri.

102. For various views on the general reliability of the tradition, *vide* S.P. Gupta and K.S. Ramachandran (eds.), *Mahābhārata: Myth and Reality: Differing Views*, including our comments.

103. Born in AD 476, Āryabhaṭa (*Āryabhaṭiya*, Kālakriyā-pāda, 10) avers that when three *pādas* of the *yuga* (viz. Kṛita, Tretā and Dvāpara) and 3600 years more had gone, twenty-three years from his birth had elapsed:

षष्ट्यब्दानां षष्टिर्यदा व्यतीतास्त्रयश्च युगपादाः ।
त्र्यधिका विंशतिरब्दास्तदेह मम जन्मनोऽतीताः ।।

104. त्रिंशत्सु त्रिसहस्रेषु भारतादाहवादितः ।
सप्ताब्दशतयुक्तेषु गतेष्वब्देषु पञ्चसु ।।
पञ्चाशत्सु कलौ काले षट्सु पञ्चशतासु च ।
समासु समतीतासु शकानामपि भूभुजाम् ।।
EI, VI, p. 7, verses 33-34.

105. आसन् मघासु मुनयः शासति पृथिवीं युधिष्ठिरे नृपतौ ।
षड्द्विकपञ्चद्वियुतः शककालस्तस्य राज्ञश्च ।।

Despite varying interpretations of the stanza (see our *Varāhamihira's India*, I, p. 34, note 45), this happens to be the only interpretation backed by tradition as seen from Kalhaṇa's *Rāja-taraṅgiṇī* as will be shown in the sequel.

106. *Vide* P.C. Sengupta, 'Astronomical References in the Mahābhārata and their

Implications', *JRASBL*, III, 1933, pp. 101-19; 'Bhārata Battle Traditions', *ibid.*, IV, 1938, pp. 393-413.

107. शतेषु षट्सु सार्धेषु त्र्यधिकेषु च भूतले।
कलेर्गतेषु वर्षाणामभूवन् कुरुपाण्डवा:।।

108. वंश्येषु तस्य नृपतिषु वर्षसहस्त्रयं पदमवाप्य।
यातेषु देवभूयं क्षितीश्वर: पुष्यवर्माऽभूत्।।
IAA, p. 41, verse 7.

109. For a discussion, see P.V. Kane, *History of Dharmśāstra*, III, pp. 898-99. However, Kane assigns an average period of twenty years per ruler and arrives at the beginning of the fifth century AD for Pushyavarman which would be too late a date for him.

110. For details, *vide* P.V. Kane, *ibid.*, pp. 898-99.

111. For a discussion of the evidence, see B.B. Lal, 'Excavations at Hastinapur and Other Explorations in the Upper Ganga and Sutlej Basin: 1950-52', *Ancient India*, Nos. 11-12, 1954-55, pp. 1-151. He found at Hastinapur a large part of the habitation of the PGW culture washed away by a flood which, to him, corroborated the Purāṇic tradition that a serious flood forced Nichakshu, son of Parīkshit, to shift his capital to Kauśāmbī. He dates this layer in the tenth century BC shortly before which the Mahābhārata war must have taken place. He dates the war itself around 900 BC. His latest contribution on the theme in 'This is how an Archaeologist Looks at the Historicity of the Mahābhārata', in Ajay Mitra Shastri (ed.), *Mahābhārata: Some Facets,* under publication. Vidha Tripathi (*Painted Grey Ware and the Iron Age Culture of Northern India,* pp.; 122-31) has summerised his views and given a list of Painted Grey Ware sites known till then. D.P. Agrawal does not attach any importance to this view and cites it only casually (*The Archaeology of India*, p. 263) and leaves the readers in dark about his own view about the association between the Ware and the players of the Mahābhārata war.

Some scholars are in favour of regarding the Harappan remains as those of the Mahābhārata age and thus pushing the archaeological date of the war to around third millnnium BC. *Vide* I.K. Sarma, 'The Mahābhārata: A Critical Study of the Archaeological Data', in Ajay Mitra Shastri (ed.), *Mahābhārata: Some Facets,* for a discussion of the evidence.

F.E. Pargiter (*Ancient Indian Historical Tradition*, pp. 175-82)) after a careful analytical assessment of the total number of reigns between Parīkshit, who succeeded Yudhishṭhira, and Mahāpadma, who founded the Nanda dynasty that preceded the Mauryas, arrives at about 950 BC for the time of the battle. However, though well-based on the Purāṇic data, his date suffers from abnormally low averages assigned to the individual reigns, viz. 18 years, and therefore deserves a review. S.B. Roy (*The Date of the Mahābhārata War*, pp. 139-48) reviews the various current theories about the date of this event and himself argues for a date about mid-fifteenth century BC (*ibid.*, pp. 116- 48), his favoured date being around 1424 BC (p. 148).

112. S.R. Rao who identifies the present Beṭ Dwārakā as the Dvārakā of the *Mahābhārata*. See his 'Marine Archaeological Investigations in Indian Waters

and Discovery of submerged Dvārakā', *Mañjūshā: Dr S.R. Rao 60th Birthday Falicitation Volume,* Bangalore, 1985, pp. 23-27; 'Excavations at the Submerged Ports: Dvārakā, A Case Study', *Marine Archaeology of the Indian Ocean Countries,* Goa, 1987, pp. 47-53.

113. For a gist of the data in these works, see M.M. Sharma, *IAA*, Introduction, pp. 8-10.

114. But in the Tezpur and Parbatiyā charters (verse 4) of Vanamālavarman (*IAA*, pp. 97 and 116) of the ninth century AD. Vajradatta is described as one of the two sons of Naraka, the other being Bhagadatta. According to this tradition, thus, Vajradatta was a (younger) brother of Bhagadatta. But this appears to be due to confusion and is untrustworthy.

115. P.C. Chowdhury, *HCPA*, p. 132.

116. Hence the following proverb:
यदिहास्ति तदन्यत्र यन्नेहास्ति न तत् क्वचित्।

117. For that matter even West Bengal or Bangladesh has neither yielded any Aśokan monument nor is mentioned in any of his records. But Yuan Chwang speaks of the presence of some monuments erected by Aśoka which may perhaps indicate its inclusion in the Maurya empire during Aśoka's time.

118. *The Kauṭilīya Arthaśāstra,* ed. R.P. Kangle, Book II, Chapter 11.

119. अगुरु जोङ्ग कालं कालचित्रं वा। ५७। श्यामं दोङ्ग कम्। ५८।
Ibid., II. 11.

120. तैलपर्णिकमशोकग्रामिकं मांसवर्ण पद्मगन्धि। ६९। जोङ्गकं रक्तपीतकमुत्पलगन्धि गोमूत्रगन्धि वा। ६२। ग्रामेरुकं स्निग्धं गोमूत्रगन्धि।६३। सौवर्णकुड्यकं रक्तपीतं मातुलुड्गगन्धि ।६४। पूर्णकद्वीपकं पद्मगन्धि नवनीतगन्धि वा ।६५।
Ibid., II.11.

121. *Bhadraśriya* looks somewhat strange and the correct form of the word might have been *bhadraśrī.*

122. भद्रश्रियं पारलौहित्यकं मांसवर्ण जातीवर्णम् ।६६। आन्तरवत्यमुशीरवर्णम् ।६७। उभयं कुष्ठगन्धि च ।६८।
Ibid., II. 11.

123. The commentators are cited in the footnotes at pp. 116-17 of R.P. Kangle's Engl. translation of *The Kauṭilīya Arthaśāstra.* We have utilised this translation.

124. *SEHA*, pp. 221-25; 232-35. The notion that Kauṭilya was a southerner has nothing to commend itself. The only thing that can be said with confidence is that he had widely travelled with an eye for every novelty of most of the regions he saw. Even otherwise the *Arthaśāstra* does not represent only his personal observations; as usual in such cases, he had collected information on varied topics from various works and persons working under him. And so he had as much knowledge of the products of South India as of the East for which reason he can not be dubbed as an easterner as well as attempted by some. *Vide ibid*., pp. 236-38.

Chapter II

INERTIA AND RESURGENCE

1. Early Evidence of Indigenous Religions in Meghalaya
2. Did Pushyamitra Śuṅga Invade Kāmarūpa ?
3. Early Foreign Contacts
4. Emergence of Varmans and the Gupta Age
5. Contacts with Other Indian Powers
6. Institution of Agrāhāras and Patronage of Vedic-Paurāṇic Learning

Appendix I . Text of the Dūbī Seal
Appendix II . The Nālandā Seal of Bhāskaravarman
Appendix III . Donees of the Nidhānpur Plates of Bhāskaravarman

1. EARLY EVIDENCE OF INDIGENOUS RELIGIONS IN MEGHALAYA

We have taken a hurried survey of the contacts that North-Eastern India had with the rest of the country up to about the Maurya period. As the time progressed, acquaintance and interaction grew considerably. Before proceeding further, we should like to invite attention to some rather recent findings which reveal that during the early centuries AD, if not before, the region now covered by the present state of Meghalaya had, like the rest of the country, become a stronghold of the Paurāṇic religion and perhaps Buddhism.

The first such report was published in 1957 where it was stated that the officers of the State Museum, Guwahati, found miscellaneous tenth-eleventh century sculptures at Devasthān, district Nowgong, and Phulbari, Garo Hills.[1] Thereafter several sporadic finds of *Śiva-liṅgas*, *Yoni-pīṭhas*, fragments of images of Paurāṇic divinities and stray remnants of temples were reported from Phulbari and Bhaitbari in the Garo Hills in Meghalaya in various newspapers and popular magazines from time to time.[2] But a systematic, even if of an extremely short duration, excavation was first carried out at Vadagokugiri, better known as Bhaitbari, in the Tura district of West Garo Hills, Meghalaya, by the Prehistory Branch of the Archaeological Survey of India, under Shri A.K. Sharma in January-March 1992. Fortunately for us, a brief account of this excavation has been published.[3] According to the excavator, this excavation has yielded dependable evidence of the occupation of the site prior to the Christian era and of a massive fortification including mud and brick mixed rampart wall with numerous bastions, a wide deep moat (*parikhā*) on the outer side of the fortification wall, and very wide gateways on all the four cardinal sides of the fortification. Three archaeological periods of this fortification could also be determined.

The remains of a possible (?) huge stūpa dating from around the first century AD and built of mud-cum-bricks in box-chamber style approached by flights of steps in the centre of these chambers were also found on the north-western fringe of the fortified township.[4]

The town appears to have had a mixed population following both Buddhism and the Paurāṇic religion as we have evidence of Hindu temples as well. At least two groups have been unearthed: one almost in the centre of the fortified township and the other on the north-western side adjoining the river-bank. Each group has at least ten to twelve mounds which, basing on the surface indications and their location, may be designated temple mounds. The first group has five tanks, the largest one being that (400 m x 180 m) on the south of the rest which are close to each other, side by side and close to the riverside. Most of the temples of the second group were located around a rectangular tank that still has plenty of water with blooming lotus and lily. All around the tanks were spotted several architectural fragments of temples like the *āmalakas*, miniature *śikharas*, decorative pieces with floral designs, lintels and door-jambs as well as *Śiva-liṅgas* with *yonis*, some of them having been collected and kept inside a makeshift bamboo structure under a huge banyan tree on the eastern embankment and still worshipped by the local Koch people as their ancestral deities. And on the top of the opposite eastern bank inside the bamboo grove are assembled several structural fragments of large lithic temples which the local Garos worship as their village deities. And several architectural members of varying dimensions and brickbats and fragments of divine figures were found lying in the adjoining area willy-nilly. The extant evidence appears to indicate that almost all the temples were wrought from bricks, and perhaps only a few from stones. And local reports indicate that practically all the mounds yielded from time to time in course of collecting wood, digging and ploughing a large number of decorated and sculptured terracotta plaques. Two big boulders engraved with the model of elevational model of the main shrine were found lying in a stream on the eastern fringe of the fortified township. These models appear to indicate a style combining the *pīḍha deul* and the *rekha deul* types, and these as well as the numerous architectural fragments revealed that at least some of the temples were built in the Orissan style with a perceptible impact of the Pratihāra style and are datable to the period roughly between the seventh and eleventh centuries AD. One of these is an octagonal Śiva temple.[5]

A large number of terracotta plaques of Paurāṇic divinities and some semi-secular personages varying in fabricating quality depending on the skill of the artists have also been reported. They include, besides *Śiva-liṅgas* and *yoni-pīṭhas* which have already been mentioned, Gaṇeśa in various poses including dancing (*nṛitya-Gaṇeśa*),[6] three-eyed Śiva,[7] Umā-Maheśvara, goddesses Kālī (dancing as well as seated), Ugra-Tārā, Sarasvatī[7a] and Vaishṇavī, Tāntrik ascetic figures (both male and female)[8], sometimes dancing, Vidyādharas[8a] and females, dancing[9] and playing on musical instruments like *mṛdaṅga.*

It would appear from the above that the ancestors of the present day Garos were adherents of indigenous Indian religions like Buddhism and Paurāṇicism which were also highly popular in other parts of India. This small-scale work with such spectacular results only underlines urgent need of more archaeological work on a larger scale in the hilly regions of the North-East which is sure to bring to light more such links and bind emotionally the local people with those elsewhere in India more intimately than hitherto.

2. DID PUSHYAMITRA ŚUNGA INVADE KĀMARŪPA ?

We have seen in the preceding lecture that the Varman kings beginning with Pushyavarman traced their descent from Naraka followed by his son Bhagadatta and grandson Vajradatta, the last two of whom played an active role in the Mahābharata war and averred that the rulers following Vajradatta ruled for three thousand years before Pushyavarman ascended the throne. This is stated for the first time in the Nidhānpur plates of Bhāskaravarman[10] who is known to have flourished in the first half of the seventh century AD. Now, the most popular traditional date of the Bhārata war, as stated above, happens to be 3102 BC. Assuming this date to be the only correct one and also the statement of the inscriptions regarding the interval of 3000 years between Vajradatta, who participated in this war, and the first known Varman king Pushyavarman to be exact, D. Sharma has suggested that Pushyavarman was only slightly later than the Śuṅga upstart Pushyamitra (flourishing about 185-150 BC) and thus placed him in the first century BC and dated his accession near about 120 BC.[11] In this conclusion he was also guided by the similarity of the names Pushyamitra and Pushyavarman pointed out by K.L. Barua.[12] He felt that in his *Raghu-vaṁśa* Kālidāsa actually had before him the victorious campaigns of Pushyamitra who had humbled an hitherto unknown Prāgjyotisha-Kāmarūpa monarch who must have preceded Pushyavarman who assumed this name only to show that he was not inferior to and could well vie with the Śuṅga rulers following Agnimitra and to declare his independence of the Magadhan power which he had now disowned.

We, too, feel that in so far as Kālidāsa is concerned, the now popular notion that he flourished in the Gupta Age, more particularly during the reign of Chandra Gupta II Vikramāditya, assumes too much and is based on very fragile data. And nothing has hitherto been produced to finally set aside his traditional date in the first century BC. On the other hand we find him choosing as the theme of his first play, *Mālavikāgnimitra*, an episode relating to the first Śuṅga king Pushyamitra and his son and successor, Agnimitra, which was not so popular as to be remembered over five centuries later to be selected by a celebrated poet-dramatist for his dramatic debut that the *Mālavikāgnimitra* undoubtedly was. And then in his poem *Megha-dūta* he speaks of Vidiśā as a capital which could be true only of the last one-and-a-half pre-Christian centuries following Pushyamitra who continued to rule from the erstwhile imperial capital at Pāṭaliputra, viz. during the post-Pushyamitra Śuṅga and Kāṇvāyana periods when the capital had been shifted to Vidisha. In view of these facts one has to think twice before rejecting the ancient tradition that placed Kālidāsa in the first century BC. But there was no necessity whatsoever for Kālidāsa to describe in his *Raghu-vaṁśa* Pushymitra's military career under the pretext of Raghu. If this were his intention, there was nothing to prevent him from referring to Pushyamitra by this very name as he had already done in his *Mālavikāgnimitra*. It would be like arguing that he described Samudra Gupta's conquests in the name of Raghu, named the *Vikramorvaśīya* after Chandra Gupta II, who had Vikrama for his *viruda*, and composed the *Kumāra-sambhava* to celebrate the birth of the latter's son Kumāra Gupta I, which are some of the gratuitous assumptions of the proponents of dating Kālidāsa during the Gupta age. We are inclined to hold that while the poet composed his poems and plays on mythological themes unless otherwise indicated explicitly, he utilised his extensive erudition including that of geography in his descriptions and no undue meaning for contemporary history ought to be sought in them.

However, even if the above date for Kālidāsa is conceded, this by itself does not establish a late second–early first century BC date for the Kāmarūpa king Pushyavarmn. As we have seen above, there prevailed different traditions concerning the date of the Mahābhārata war, and 3102 BC, though most popular, was just one of the prevailing dates for the event. And the statement in the Nidhānpur copperplate charter of Bhāskaravarman, which happens to be the only one to contain it, that three thousand years had elapsed from Vajradatta to the accession of Pushyavarman can not be taken to refer to the exact number of years. Such statements, specially when alluding to millennia, must be taken as referring to years in the round or just rough period counted from a particular happening. And it was quite a popular practice to refer to time in round figures from specified events like the birth or *parinirvāṇa* of Mahāvīra or Buddha or even from Nandarāja, the last one met with in the famous Hāthīgumphā inscription of the Kaliṅga emperor Khāravela.[13] Therefore one can not be sure if the mention of 3000 years in the Nidhānpur plates is to be taken as exact; it is more likely to be an indication of a long time elapsed between the two events in question, especially when the lapse of a long period had resulted in factual confusion.

And the inscriptional evidence leaves no doubt about Pushyavarman being succeeded by his son Samudravarman, and no strong evidence has been adduced to sustain the supposition that some generations intervened between the two.[14] And as far as king Surendravarman brought to historical notice by the Umāchal Rock Inscription is concerned, we are inclined to take him as a collateral member of the line who need not be equated with any other known monarch of the Varman line beginning with Pushyavarman.[15] In short, we may conclude that as of now there is absolutely nothing to sustain any involvement of Pushyamitra Śuṅga in the affairs of Prāgjyotisha-Kāmarūpa and the unknown predecessor of Pushyavarman being compelled to concede his tutelage and Pushyavarman adopting the name with a view to disown Śuṅga sovereignty and to demonstrate his equality with the Śuṅga victor. However, Kālidāsa's description of Raghu's campaign against Prāgjyotisha, a few stanzas later called Kāmarūpa, does show that an erudite North Indian poet was aware of the power and economic wealth of the North-East which was an inseparable part of an all-India expedition (*digvijaya*) as early as the first century BC as was previously the case with some of the Mahābhārata heroes.

3. EARLY FOREIGN CONTACTS

Attention may now be invited to certain early Chinese and classical allusions which shed important light on the economy and inhabitants of the North-East. In the second century BC. Manipur appears to have served as a station of trade between India and China by the land-route. According to the information supplied by the *Ma-twa-lin*, in about 125 BC the Chinese general Chang-kien, who was sent on a mission by the Chinese emperor to Ta-hia (viz. Bactria), was astonished to see there canes of the Khiong reed and cloth of Shu. He was told by the people that their (Bactrians') merchants were sent to buy these commodities to Shin-tu or India, and Mo-kie-tho (Magadha) is specifically named in this context.[16] These were actually transported from Yunnān to Madhyadeśa (the Middle Country) through Manipur and thence to Bactria by the then Grand Route. It must, of course, be admitted that this land-route was not in popular use during the period owing to serious difficulties involved.

Some of the classical writers make interesting allusions to some of the peoples, commercial products and trading practices of the North-East. The first among these is the *Periplus maris Erythraei*, better known to South Asian historians as the *Periplus of the Erythrean Sea*, composed by an anonymous Greek sailor settled in Egypt in the form of a diary of his voyage by maritime route from Egypt to India.[17] Its date has been a subject of keen controversy among scholars, but there is enough internal evidence to show that it was composed sometime in the latter half of the first century AD.[18] It speaks of the people called Kirrhadae (also spelt as Cirrhadae),[19] who answer the Kirātas of Indian literary and epigraphic tradition, and inhabited, *inter alia*, parts of North-Eastern India as well as the region now included in Bangladesh.[20] It also refers to a country called Chryse and its people Chryse which have been located variously by scholars. We are told that from the region known as Masalia[21] the course of the voyage lay eastward across the neighbouring bay to Desarene and thence by a northerly route passing through a variety of barbarous tribes[22] and then again to the east sailing with the ocean to one's right one reached the Ganges and the extremity of the continent[23] towards the east called Chryse (the Golden Chersonese).[24] The description is rather confusing leading scholars to widely differing locations. Thus, Taylor locates it in Arakan and Pegu as well as probably Malaccā and Sumātrā,[25] while McCrindle equates it with Malaccā[26] and Whiteley with the Malay Peninsula.[27] However, it appears to have covered a much wider region as, according to Pomponiuus Mela (III. 7. 70), it lay off the Ganges. We therefore are in agreement with P.C. Choudhury in taking it as the name of the wider area including large parts of ancient Prāgjyotisha and South-East Asia.[28] The *Periplus* further informs us that the Ganges in this region had a mart called, after it, Gange through which passed a considerable traffic consisting of betel, the Gangetic spikenard, pearls, and the finest of muslins which were also known as Gangetic. In this locality, he goes on to say, there was said to have been a gold mine and a gold coin called *Caltis*.[29] This description goes well with the North-Eastern region which has been well-known for these products since antiquity. As for gold, it reminds one of Kauṭilya's *Arthaśāstra* which speaks of Suvarnakuḍya which the commentators locate in Kāmarūpa and was, as indicated by the name, most probably an important source of superior quality of gold. And the river Brahmaputra is known to carry water with sufficient gold content which was extracted by the people. Some inscriptions bear testimony to this fact. Thus, we are told in the Tezpur grant of Vanamāladevavarman that the river Lauhitya carried down gold-dust from the boulders of the Kailāsa mountain,[30] a statement repeated in his only other known charter, viz. the Parbatīyā plates, as well.[31] The gold-washers popularly known as *Sonavāls* continued their activity till late times and during as late as the Ahom period it provided employment to a large number of people[32] besides being a major source of revenue to the state. Then, the coin called Caltis by the *Periplus*, which was in currency in Chryse, may have been connected with the people of the North-East known as Kalitā as conjectured by some scholars; it may be noted though that no such coin has been reported as yet.

The *Periplus* refers to a people called Sesatai who are commonly identified with the various peoples of the North-East including Garos of Meghalaya, Kuki-Chinas and Nagās of Nagaland.[33] We find a graphic account of a very strange trade practice in vogue among them.[34]

It is also likely that the city or region called Thina or This by the *Periplus*[35] had also to do something with the North-East and reminds one of the concluding part of the name Prāgjyotisha though most scholars locate it in Western China.[36] This is also vouched for by the connection into which it is brought with the Sesatai who held an annual fair on its border and, as we have just seen, are located by most of the scholars in the North-East. It is likely that the name (Thina) refers to the Chīnas referred to as one of the people residing in Prāgjyotisha and forming the armed forces of Bhagadatta as referred to in the *Mahābhārata*. And as the Chinese elements were present in the population of the bordering areas of the North-East, we need not go all the way to China in search of the Thinai as done by most of the Occidental scholars.

Another important name that figures in classical literature right from the time of Strabo and Pliny is Seres which denotes the inhabitants of the country of the same name. The country is also spoken of as Serica by one Kallisthenes, referred to as pseudo-Kallisthenes to distinguish him from the earlier scholar of this name who was the nephew of Aristotle.[37] Strabo refers to Seric fabrics as made from some sorts of byssus bark, by combing the fibres,[38] and McCrindle takes them to be silk-webs imported from China,[39] though it ought to be interpreted as referring to Assam silk which is mentioned by several other classical writers and is still a coveted fabric in great demand all over India. Gaius Plinius Secundus (*c.* AD 23-79), better known as Pliny, tells us that Rachia, an ambassador from Palaesimundus or Taprobane (Ceylon), paid a visit to the court of the Roman emperor Claudius and reported that his countrymen were familiar with the Seres through commerce and that his father had often gone to their country which lay close to the Hemodi (perhaps Himalaya) mountain.[40] He also refers to an interesting trade practice obtaining among them.[41] Ptolemy in his *Treatise on Geography*, composed around AD 150,[42] refers to the country and its people, both called Seres,[43] which Taylor has ably demonstrated to correspond to the plains and hills of the Assam region.[44] Its correctness is vouched for by other sources which refer to its various commercial products and other practices. Strabo says that the country of Seres abounded in elephants which is true of the North-East even now. Several other sources aver that silk was produced by the Seres which is still true, and *mūṁgā* and *tasar* silks are still well-known products of this region. Ammianus speaks of silk from Seres called Sericum which was exported to other lands. He also mentions skin, iron, aloe, musk and rhinoceros' horns as common products of this region. Most of these are still commonly produced in this region, and in particular rhinoceros is much more common here than anywhere else in India. According to Ptolemy, to the east of Serica there were hills and forests where canes were grown in abundance and used for bridges which can still be observed in this region where, in spite of enormous growth of bridge-building techniques, people even now continue to employ bamboos as bridges. Some of the rivers mentioned by the classical writers may also be equated with those flowing in this region.[45]

What is of particular interest in this connection is the fact that most of the Graeco-Roman writers speak of this region in course of their account of India and know of its close commercial relations with the other parts of India with which it was physically connected by numerous routes which were frequented by traders and other entrepreneurs.

4. EMERGENCE OF THE VARMANS AND THE GUPTA AGE

As we have seen, most of the ruling families of Prāgjyotisha trace their origin from Vishṇu in his Boar (Varāha) incarnation and the earth goddess (bhūmi) through their progeny Naraka and the latter's son and grandson Bhagadatta and Vajradatta respectively. But most of the historians naturally doubt the veracity of these traditions and postulate theories placing Naraka or Bhagadatta at some or other point in a couple of centuries BC or early centuries AD. D. Sharma is of the opinion that there were as many as three monarchs bearing the name Naraka all of whom ruled in the western region beyond the river Brahmaputra and the last of them migrated from the Videha region and established himself in Prāgjyotisha. And all this happened prior to the traditional Bhagadatta of the Mahābhārata period.[46] It is certainly possible as well as imperative to think so in view of the fact that early as well as mediaeval Sanskrit writers have confused several personages of the name Naraka and converted them into one just because of the identity of names which was very common in those days. But except for only some late traditions in such late texts as the *Kālikā-purāṇa* and the *Yoginī-tantra* there is hardly anything to vouch for Naraka's association with king Janaka of Videha or Mithilā. However, as Sharma does not place him within the time-bracket in question, we have in the present context not much to do with his standpoint on this issue. B.N. Kakati, however, places Naraka sometime between AD 200 and 500.[47] The latter part of this time-bracket (AD 500) is squarely opposed to known historical facts as Pushyavarman, whose descent is traced from him and from his son Bhagadatta, is known to have flourished early in the fourth century AD.[48] P.C. Chowdhury, however, treats Naraka as a historical personage[49] and takes Naraka-Bhagadatta as the dynastic title.[50]

The first historically documented dynasty of Prāgjyotisha to lay claim to this hallowed lineage was that traditionally called Bhauma,[51] Vārāha[52] and Nāraka[53] and more popularly known to historians as Varman[54] which rose to power early in the fourth century AD and once again placed the region on the pan-Indian map politically and culturally. This tradition is recorded in the Dūbī[55] and the Nidhānpur[56] plates of its last known member Bhāskaravarman,[57] who flourished in the first half of the seventh century AD. These plates narrate how king Naraka was born of the contact between the Varāha (boar manifestation of Vishṇu) and the earth goddess when he rescued her from the ocean, how he turned wicked and had to be destroyed by Kṛishṇa, was followed by his son Bhagadatta and grandson Vajradatta in succession. Vajradatta devoted himself to learning and performed several Aśvamedha sacrifices. He was followed by several other kings after whom Pushyavarman came to power. And thereafter his lineal descendants up to Bhāskaravarman are eulogised. The legends on the two hitherto known seals of Bhāskaravarman, one attached to his Dūbī plates[58] and the other found at the famous Buddhistic centre of Nālandā,[59] also afford the official genealogy commencing with Pushyavarman who is hailed as belonging to the lineage of Bhagadatta and Vajradatta.[60] A similar account, though beginning with a later king, Bhūtivarman, who ruled a few generations after Pushyavarman, is given by the celebrated litterateur Bāṇabhaṭṭa in his *Harsha-charita* (*Biography of Harsha*). Haṁsavega, Bhāskaravarman's envoy to Harsha of Sthāṇvīśvara (modern Thanesar, Kurukshetra district, Haryana) and Kānykubja (modern Kannauj, Farrukhabad district, Uttar Pradesh), is reported to have told the latter that in olden times by the contact of god Mahāvarāha goddess earth conceived and gave birth to Naraka who was very powerful and even gods became afraid of him. In his lineage came Bhagadatta, Pushpadatta and Vajradatta. And after several other kings had ruled, Bhūtivarman came to power.[61] Obviously, Bhūtivarman was more important and powerful as compared to his predecessors beginning with Pushyavarman mentioned in the dynasty's own inscriptions and seals notwithstanding the fact that he is styled just *mahārāja* as against *mahārājādhirāja* in the family's official records.

But a **fact of great historical value** that emerges from a careful study of the seal-inscriptions is that **Pushyavarman was the (or a) son of a personage named Naraka** as the former is styled *Naraka-tanaya* in the very beginning. The word *tanaya* has baffled the historians who have attempted to explain it away variously. D.C. Sircar takes it to have been employed in the secondary sense of a 'male descendant' in preference to its primary sense of 'son'.[62] M.M. Sharma, on the other hand, renders it by 'a grandson'[63] without any justification. D. Sharma is better though in a much more queer situation and takes it as an adjective of the following expression *Bhagadatta-Vajradatt-ānvayaḥ* and renders the two expressions together as 'a descendant of the lineage of Bhagadatta and Vajradatta born from Naraka',[64] glossing over the fact that the expression *Naraka-tanaya* is employed as an adjective of Pushyavarman. All these renderings are caused by the difficulty of accommodating it with the tradition which makes Naraka the first male ancestor of the dynastic line. But in natural course there ought to be no difficulty as there could in the same line be more than a single personage of the same name as we find in several other dynasties and ordinary families.[65] And it was actually a common practice to name children after their renowned ancestors. In view of such a vogue it would have been extremely strange if this name (Naraka) was not given to any of his descendants. Thus there was a personage named Naraka in the family of the homonymous progenitor in end-third century–early fourth century AD whose son was Pushyavarman. This Naraka was, however, a person of not much standing or power as indicated by his non-mention in the stereotyped *praśasti* in the two inscriptions of Bhāskaravarman under reference as well as by the nature of his mention in the two seal-inscriptions.

The whole expression reads either *śrīman=Naraka-tanayo Bhagadatta-Vajradatt-ānvayo* or with the initial word as *śrīmān*. The reading in the Nālandā seal-inscription is clearly *śrīman*,[66] whereas D.C. Sircar reads the same word on the Dūbī seal as *śrīmān*.[67] If the desired reading is actually the former (*śrīman*), it would be applicable to Naraka who would then be intended to be referred to as 'illustrious' or (literally) as 'endowed with prosperity', and if the latter were to be accepted as correct it would refer to his son Pushyavarman. However, the latter personage is clearly referred to immediately after this expression as *mahārājādhirāja-śrī-Prāgjyotish-endra* and consequently the employment of an additional *śrīmat* for him would be simply redundant. We are therefore inclined to hold that the intended reading in the text of the Dūbī seal, too, was *śrīman*, and not *śrīmān* as read by Sircar and, following him, others. Unfortunately, the facsimile of the relevant portion and a few subsequent lines in the Dūbī seal accompanying Sircar's paper as also that reproduced by some others is not clear and our efforts to verify it have also not been successful.[68] But we feel strongly that even if the reading of the word in question on the Dūbī seal is in fact *śrīmān*, it must be an error for *śrīman* which would make a good sense, and such errors are not quite uncommon in early Indian epigraphs. Whatever that be, there is no doubt left that Naraka was a rather insignificant person; he is, in fact, the only member of the family mentioned without any regal title whereas all the rest are styled *mahārājādhirāja* or so intended. It is evident therefore that he had no regal pretension.[68a]

Before proceeding further it would be helpful to give the genealogy and order of succession of the Varmans as gleaned from the two charters and seal-inscriptions of Bhāskaravarman and the *Harsha-charita* of Bāṇa:

King	*Chief Queen*
(Naraka)	
Pushyavarman	
Samudravarman	Dattadevī
Balavarman	Ratnavatī
Kalyāṇavarman	Gandharvavatī
Gaṇapativarman	Yajñavatī
Mahendravarman	Suvratā
Nārāyaṇavarman	Devavatī
Bhūtivarman	Vijñānavatī
Chandramukhavarman	Bhogavatī
Sthitavarman	Nayanadevī
Susthitavarman	Śyāmādevī
Supratishṭhitavarman	Bhāskaravarman[69]

This is just the genealogy and order of succession based on the descriptions met with in the Dūbī[70] and Nidhānpur[71] plates of Bhāskaravarman excluding only the founder of the family named Naraka who is mentioned in his seal-inscriptions alone. These include also a collateral member, viz. Supratishṭhitavarman, elder brother of Bhāskaravarman, who, however, finds no place in the description encountered in Bāṇa's *Harsha-charita* and the inscription on the seal attached to Bhāskaravarman's own Dūbī charter. It is pertinent to note in this context that though the text of this copper plate charter refers to him in glowing terms, he finds no mention in the legend on the seal affixed to these plates. And the same must have evidently been the case with the seal affixed to the Nidhānpur charter which is, however, not forthcoming. There is nothing absolutely to be surprised at this omission as he happened to be a collateral member of the family even though he, too, became king immediately before Bhāskaravarman. Collaterals are often not referred to in official genealogy. There are, of course, exceptions like the Sonepat and Bānskherā seals of emperor Harshavardhana which contain a reference to his elder brother and royal predecessor Rājyavardhana, and the Nālandā seal (or sealing) of Bhāskaravarman also does the same. No special significance need therefore be attached to mention or non-mention of an elder brother who may or may not have ascended the throne. It depended entirely on the nature of relations between the two and was left purely to the fancy of the king or the composer of the seal-inscription.

The rulers from Pushyavarman to Kalyāṇavarman are styled *mahārājādhirāja* in the seal-inscriptions,[72] while the rest right up to Bhāskaravarman are named without any regal title. But there should be no doubt that this omission is due to inadvertence on the part of the composer of the legends and that the kings who followed Kalyāṇavarman were also intended to be given the same imperial style. It might, however, appear doubtful if these early rulers up to Kalyāṇavarman were powerful enough to bear this title or it was attributed to them by Bhāskaravarman[73] during whose time the Prāgjyotisha kings had certainly attained an imperial status. That this style did not reflect the actual position as regards the early members of the dynasty and that they did not really assume it might appear from the fact that Haṁsavega, Bhāskaravarman's envoy to Harsha, in the message from his master did not use it for even Bhūtivarman, who was separated from Kalyāṇavarman by three generations (Gaṇapativarman, Mahendravarman and Nārāyaṇavarman all of whom came to throne in this order), and referred to him only as *mahārāja* which is an inferior title applicable to rather insignificant ruling chiefs[74] during the age in question, and it is only his great-grandson Susthiravarman who is for the first time accorded the imperial title *mahārājādhirāja*.[75] Thus, if one were to go by Bāṇa, one might regard it as almost certain that the title was deliberately given to the earlier members of the dynasty during the reign of Bhāskaravarman when the family had already attained the imperial status and that the earlier rulers were not that great as it might appear from the application of this title to them in the seal-inscriptions belonging to him. However, that either Haṁsavega was not acquainted with the actual facts of earlier history of his master's family or that his message is not correctly reported in the *Harsha-charita* would follow from the fact that the Baḍagaṅgā stone inscription of Bhūtivarman employs this style in combination with the titles *parama-daivata* and *parama-bhaṭṭāraka* for him. Moreover, as we learn from this inscription, he had performed at least one Aśvamedha sacrifice (*aśvamedha-yājin*) which is indicative of his high political ambition and sovereign status. Moreover, Mahendravarman (Bhūtivarman's grandfather) before him and Sthiravarman (Bhūtivarman's grandson) after him had performed two, not one, horse-sacrifices and are styled as *dvisturaga-medh-āhartṛ* and *dviraśvamedha-yājin* respectively in the seal-inscriptions. It would therefore follow that at least most of the early kings of Prāgjyotisha were sovereign rulers without being required to acknowledge, at least formally, any other superior authority. It is possible, however, that the predecessors of Mahendravarman did not in fact assume this imperial style and that it is applied to them in Bhāskara's records either to show them reverence or out of ignorance of the facts or because the composer of the record then could not just believe that they were subordinates to some other superior power.[75a]

In addition to these thirteen Prāgjyotisha kings known from the seal-inscriptions as well as the aforesaid two charters of Bhāskaravarman we must account for a certain Surendravarman who has been brought to notice by his own Umāchal[76] (near Guwahati) rock inscription.[77] The object of the inscription was to record probably his pious act of excavating a cave (viz. cave-shrine) in honour of Balabhadra.[78] He is known only from this epigraph wherein he is styled *mahārājādhirāja*. That he, too, belonged to the dynasty under reference need not be doubted, for the area round Guwahati over which he enjoyed authority was during this period held by the members of this line and there could be no question of a chief belonging to any other line ruling over this region during the same time. This is admitted on all hands, but finding a place for him has posed a tough problem for epigraphists and historians alike. D.C. Sircar and P.D. Chaudhury, who edited this epigraph, proposed to equate him with Mahendravarman on the ground that Mahendra and Surendra both denote god Indra and that Sanskrit writers were very fond of using synonymous words even in personal names.[79] But it has to be remembered in this context that this practice was resorted to mostly due to metrical exigencies while the inscription in question is couched in prose where there could be no question whatever of any such compulsion. It is pertinent to note that even though the Dūbi and Nidhānpur charters of Bhāskaravarman are composed in verses where there might be the possibility of employing synonyms for names owing to metrical difficulties, the name is found as it is (Mahendra). Then again, prosodically there is no difference between the two words as both have an identical number of metrical components. And his two seal-inscriptions give almost the same forms of names without any major alteration in prose. We have therefore to take the name Surendravarman as it is and try to accommodate him in the dynastic list. As palaeographically the inscription is close to the Baḍagaṅgā inscription of Bhūtivarman, Umāchal epigraph and Surendravarman brought to light by the latter have to be dated about the same time. Whether he was a rebel or a collateral ruler, which would amply account for his non-mention in the records of Bhāskaravarman, is difficult to determine in the present state of inadequate information.

Next as to the date of the emergence of this dynasty. Bhāskaravarman, the last known member of the family, was a contemporary of Harshavardhana who is known to have lived in the first half of the seventh century AD. This contemporaneity is based on Bāṇa's *Harsha-charita* and the Chinese pilgrim Yuan Chwang's travelogue and the latter's *Biography* by Shaman Hwui Li to which we shall advert later. It is also definite that the *Harsha-charita* was finished early in Harsha's reign as it is reticent about important political events of his reign including his conflict with the Gauḍa king Śaśāṅka which took place sometime around AD 620.[80] Its composition may therefore be dated prior to this date.[81]

Bhāskaravarman, whose messenger Haṁsavega had met him in one of the early stages of his march against Śaśāṅka, was already on the throne and perhaps felt threatened by the menacing postures of the same ambitious Gauḍa king which made him seek the friendship of the Pushyabhūti king. Therefore it may be presumed with enough justification that he had ascended the throne at the latest around the beginning of the seventh century AD,[82] if not earlier as supposed by some. With this approximate date for the accession of Bhāskaravarman, the last known member of the dynasty, we may proceed to fix the approximate date for the emergence of this family with the accession of its first known king Pushyavarman.[83] Now, Bhāskaravarman was preceded by thirteen rulers of his line including twelve known from his own records and Surendravarman brought to light by his Umāchal rock inscription. However, as Surendravarman might have been a rebel ruling concurrently with some other Varman king (or kings), he may be left out of account for the present purpose. We have therefore to consider only twelve reigns for ascertaining the approximate date for the accession of Pushyavarman as well as the emergence of the family's power.

Now, allowing on an average twenty-three years for a reign[84] we reach about AD 325 for the accession of Pushyavarman and the rise of the Varman dynasty beginning with him. This is only an approximate date and if we take the fact that some of the kings must have ruled for a shorter or longer period as natural, we may only aver that Pushyavarman ascended the throne about the end of the first quarter or early in the second quarter of the fourth century AD.[85] If a little less length (20 years or so) is given to a regin, we may roughly date the accession of pushyavarman to about mid-fourth century AD. In any case it can't be dated much later.

Mention must now be made of the Allahabad pillar inscription of the Gupta emperor Samudra Gupta which informs us that the bordering powers[86] including the kings of Samataṭa, Ḍavāka, Kāmarūpa, Nepal and Kartṛipura gratified the terrible commands of the emperor by giving him all the taxes, obeying his orders and visiting (the Gupta court) for paying him obeisance.[87] Two of these kings, viz. of Ḍavāka and Kāmarūpa, belonged to ancient Prāgjyotisha. This description has been debated hotly by historians, and there is difference of opinion about their identity. There is no doubt about the equation of Kāmarūpa which, as we have seen earlier, referred primarily to the region round Guwahati and it was later that with the expansion of the authority of its rulers it came to connote a much larger area. However, as regards Ḍavāka, there is some uncertainty. V.A. Smith locates it round about the districts of Bogra, Dinajpur and Rajshahi in modern Banglades,[88] whereas R.S. Tripathi places it in the Dhaka or the hilly region of the Chittagong (Chitragrāma) district in the same country.[89] Gerini equates it with Ptolemy's Dobassai in upper Myanmar.[90] But all these equations are wide of the mark. There is ample evidence in the Chinese sources for its location in the valley of the river Kapli in the Nowgong (Sanskrit Navagrāma) district of the present state of Assam. There still exists a locality called Ḍobok in this district which might have served as the headquarters of this kingdom.

However, while we know absolutely nothing about the ruling family of Ḍavāka or Ḍobok, we know of a whole line of the kings of Prāgjyotisha or Kāmarūpa which flourished during the time of the Guptas and for over a century thereafter, as we have just seen. But there is an astounding divergence of opinion regarding the identity of the king under reference. A definite solution of this question, however, hinges on the date of the accession of Samudra Gupta and the settlement of the problem as to who initiated the Gupta era: Chandra Gupta I or Samudra Gupta. Historians have generally been crediting the former with the foundation of the reckoning to mark his assumption of sovereign status marked by his adoption of the superior regal style *mahārājādhirāja* instead of the rather inferior title *mahārāja* borne by his two predecessors. But the era does not appear to have been started deliberately[91] as the era had yet to get a name even during the initial years of his homonymous grandson, viz. Chandra Gupta II, as would follow from its mention as an 'era coming down from (earlier) time' (*kāl-ānuvartamāna-saṁvatsara*) in the earliest hitherto known record of his reign, viz. Mathurā pillar inscription of the sixty-first year of this reckoning which corresponded to the fifth year from his accession.[92] If the era was really started by Chandra Gupta I to celebrate his throwing off the yoke of some other ruler, he must have ruled thereafter for just a few years. V.A. Smith[93] and A.S. Altekar,[94] who are of this opinion, date the termination of his rule about AD 330, just about a decade after the commencement of the Gupta era. John Allan, who regards the era as coming into being as a result of the continuation of Chandra Gupta I's regnal years by his successors, also thinks that his rule must have terminated about AD 335,[95] and the date of his son Samudra Gupta's accession must fall about this time. That Chandra Gupta I did not rule for a long time is clearly indicated by the comparative rarity of his coins as well as by his confining himself to a single type (commonly known as Chandra Gupta-Kumāradevī type) throughout his rule. Some others date the event (termination of Chandra Gupta I's reign) and the following accession of his son and successor Samudra Gupta much later, say around AD 340 or 350[96] or 355[97], quite unreasonably as the resultant short reign (just about two decades according to the last view) of the latter would not have sufficed for the numerous astounding military attainments described so very graphically by Harisheṇa and for the observance of at least two horse-sacrifices inferable from his Aśvamedha type coins as well as from the Puṇe plates of the Vākāṭaka queen Prabhāvatī Guptā.[98] In view of these facts it is very likely that the era actually started from the commencement of Samudra Gupta's reign as strongly pleaded by several historians including such stalwarts as R.C. Majumdar[99] and D.C. Sircar.[100] Whatever that be, Samudra Gupta must have commenced his rule at the latest around early in the second quarter of the fourth century AD, if not earlier.

Now we may attempt the identification of the Kāmarūpa contemporary of Samudra Gupta. According to some scholars, the Kāmarūpa king contemporary to Samudra Gupta was Samudravarman. Thus, R.G. Basak is of the opinion that Pushyavarman was a contemporary of Chandra Gupta I and his son Samudravarman of the Gupta emperor Samudra Gupta,[101] a view followed by H.C. Ray[102] and some others. Some scholars even think that Balavarman, one of the Āryāvarta kings worsted by the Gupta emperor, was identical with the homonymous Kāmarūpa king who was Pushyavarman's grandson. N.N. Vasu, for instance, dates Pushyavarman in *c.* AD 275-300 and holds that his grandson Balavarman was defeated by Samudra Gupta.[103] This view has found favour with a few other historians including K.N. Dikshit,[104] N.K. Bhattasali[105] and D.R. Bhandarkar[106] also. But this equation, besides being anachronistic, is untenable for some other reasons as well. This Balavarman was an Āryāvarta king and was completely uprooted and his kingdom annexed to the Gupta empire as in the case of other kings of the group whereas the descendants of the Balavarman of Kāmarūpa continued to rule for quite a few generations. Moreover, Harisheṇa clearly distinguishes the Kāmarūpa and other bordering kings (*pratyanta-nṛipatis*) from the ruling powers of Āryāvarta which renders the suggested identification just impossible. Moreover, the fact that Pushyavarman's son and successor Samudravarman had the same name as of the Gupta emperor under reference and his chief queen also bore exactly the name of the latter's chief queen casts further doubt on the veracity of this equation and the affinity is too close to be dismissed as merely a coincidence. They must have been given these names by their father and father-in-law respectively who, in the instant case, was Pushyavarman to express his highest reverence for his contemporary Gupta emperor.[107]

There is no doubt left by the Allahabad pillar inscription that Samudra Gupta's contemporary Kāmarūpa king, Pushyavarman, acted like a subordinate chief. However, scholars differ if this was due to his having been worsted by Samudra Gupta in battle or otherwise. K.L. Barua in this connection drew scholarly attention to the local traditions which tell us about a king of the Naraka dynasty named Subāhu who had detained the sacrificial horse of king Vikramāditya who then invaded Kāmarūpa and put Subāhu to flight. Barua felt that Subāhu might have been the popular name of Pushyavarman like Mṛigāṅka was of his descendant Susthiravarman. He further conjectured that Subāhu-Pushyavarman stopped the horse and had in consequence to fight and was worsted by Vikramāditya-Samudra Gupta and had to acknowledge the Gupta suzerainty.[108] But the equation of Pushyavarman with the traditional king Subāhu is a matter of debate[109] and the date proposed for Pushyavarman's accession (*c.* AD 380) falls at least a few years posterior to the ascertained termination of Samudra Gupta's reign.[110] These are enough to show the utter untenability of this theory. It is also incongruous with the evidence of the Prayāga *praśasti* inasmuch as it makes no mention of the Gupta emperor's fight with the Kāmarūpa king as well as other *pratyanta-nṛipatis* who appear to have submitted to him of their own accord out of fear and awe without bearing the brunt of his arms and their relations with Samudra Gupta were those of a bit short of vassalage. What appears to be the fact is that Pushyavarman himself, though professedly a scion of the line of Naraka and Bhagadatta, was originally without any regal pretension being the (or a) son of a rather ordinary personage called Naraka after the traditional progenitor of the line and was propped up as a king by Samudra Gupta. In this he was prompted as much by Pushyavarman's hallowed lineage as by obvious political considerations. It was quite natural for him to feel highly obliged and grateful to the Gupta emperor which he ostensibly vented by christening (or re-christening)[111] his son and successor Samudravarman and the latter's chief queen Dattādevī after the Gupta emperor and his chief queen respectively.[112] This position is in general agreement with that of R.C. Majumdar,[113] but we do not feel that he is justified in referring to Pushyavarman as a Gupta 'feudatory' and we prefer to call him a 'subordinate ally'.[114]

It is held by some that the Pushyamitras, who are reported to have brought calamity to the Gupta empire towards the end of Kumāra Gupta's reign and were finally vanquished with great difficulty by his son and successor Skanda Gupta, were descendants of Pushyavarman.[115] This is just an example of gratuitous historical assumptions and attempts at theorising on a very slender base; for, first of all, the reading of the relevant portion in the Bhitari pillar inscription (verse 4) of Skanda Gupta[116] referring to this calamity is doubtful in the extreme, some reading it as *Pushyamitrāṁś cha*[117] and others stoutly disputing it and pleading for the reading *yudhy-amitrāñś cha*[118] and thus taking it to refer to the enemies in general, and not the Pushyamitras, who had wrought such a great disaster with their huge resources in manpower and treasury and were finally vanquished by Skanda Gupta. Let us state that the relevant letters (*pushya* or *yudhya*) are just not preserved well and the suggested restorations of these lost characters depend on one's fancy. To us the latter reading appears more likely. And even if the reference actually were to the Pushyamitras, the deployment of the plural number should indicate that they were a republican or nondescript people and not a monarchy as it would have been the case if they had descended from Pushyavarman. And then also the alleged relationship between the two would be based just on the sameness of the first component of the two names, and there would be a much greater justification in averring that the Pushyamitras of the Bhitari pillar inscription were descendants of the Śuṅga king Pushyamitra. Then, we have in some Purāṇic texts allusion to a people called Pushyamitras in the Mekalā (Maikal hills, Madhya Pradesh) region[119] far away from Kāmarūpa and if the enemies of Skanda Gupta are really referred to as Pushyamitras, they would be far better claimants for this honour.

We may now refer to those of the Prāgjyotisha kings who are known, either from their own records or from those of their descendants, to have performed the politically ambitious Aśvamedha sacrifice. There are three such kings, viz. Mahendravarman, Bhūtivarman and Sthiravarman. Of these, the first and third are said to have observed two of these sacrifices each in Bhāskaravarman's

Dūbī[120] and Nalanda[121] seals and the second one is described in his own Baḍagaṅgā rock inscription as the observer of a horse-sacrifice.[122] There has been some debate regarding the applicability of the expression *dvis-turagamedh-āharttā* occurring in line 6 of the Dūbī and line 5 of the Nalanda seal. Most scholars hold rightly that the expression is deployed for the king Mahendra or Mahendravarman who is named just before.[123] D.C. Sircar, however, disputes it and feels that the allusion is to Nārāyaṇavarman whose name follows. And thus it is Nārāyaṇavarman, not Mahendravarman, who is described as observing two Aśvamedhas. In view of its importance we may discuss the question at some length. Whereas the Baḍagaṅgā inscription speaks of the performance of the horse-sacrifice by Bhūtivarman and there is no independent contemporary evidence for the staging of this sacrifice by Mahendravarman and the seal-inscriptions would, in case the commonly held opinion is conceded, appear to be reticent on the Aśvamedha of Bhūtivarman, Sircar is inclined to hold that the reference in question in the seals is actually to Nārāyaṇavarman whose name figures next. And he further feels that it is likely that the second of the two Aśvamedhas said to have been observed by Nārāyaṇavarman was celebrated when that king was too old and his son Bhūtivarman was ruling the country on his father's behalf and that this was the reason why the latter is said to have observed an Aśvamedha in his own record.[124] He argues that even as the expression *dvir-aśvamedha-yājī* referring to the two horse-sacrifices performed by Sthiravarman precedes his name[125] so also the earlier phrase referring to the similar feat ought to be taken to refer to the following king Nārāyaṇavarman. Some force in this argument notwithstanding, we must remember the difference in the nature of the two references: while in the first case the expression *dvir aśvamedhayājī* precedes the king's name immediately, in the second instance the two (*dvis turagamedh-āharttā* and *śrī-Nārāyaṇavarmmā*) are separated by *śrī-Suvratāyāṁ* which is the name (Suvratā) of the chief queen of Mahendravarman mentioned in the locative singular, which makes a lot of difference in our understanding even though according to Sanskrit syntax any word or name could have occupied any place in a sentence. But this laxity was permissible for versified compositions to meet the metrical exigencies which, however, is not the case with the two seal-inscriptions in question which are composed entirely in prose.

That Mahendravarman had really observed some sacrifices is also vouched for by his description in the Dūbī[126] and Nidhānpur[127] charters of Bhāskaravarman which contain references to some of his sacrificial activities. While the former speaks of his observing 'a number of sacrifices like the great Indra', the latter refers to him as 'the support for sacrificial rites like the fire, the very foundation for sacrificial rites, in the manner of the friction-wood (*araṇi*), which is also the source of sacrifices (*yajñavatī*)'.[128] These references in ordinary course may have been treated as merely conventional, but they assume historical value when we find him represented as performing a couple of Aśvamedhas. That Bhūtivarman also performed a horse-sacrifice is quite certain in view of his assumption of the style *aśvamedha-yājin*, but that need not come in the way of his grandfather Mahendravarman observing the same sacrifices. The omission of reference to the former's Aśvamedha (or Aśvamedhas if he performed more than one such sacrifice) can be dismissed as due to callousness on the part of the composer of the seal-inscriptions which is also responsible for the non-specification of the regal style for many of the later members of the dynasty. Whether these Aśvamedhas were elaborate and long-drawn ones as those staged by Samudra Gupta[129] or normal ones can not be determined for want of requisite evidence. But there is no doubt that they signify the performers' attempts to assert their authority over the whole of Prāgjyotisha and to throw off whatever remained of the Gupta impact besides indicating great attachment to the Vedic-Paurāṇic religious tradition. In any case we know that by the time of Bhūtivarman (*c.* AD 500-525) the Nowgong region where Ḍavāka was situated and the Surma valley (Sylhet district and adjoining area in the present Bangladesh) where the land originally donated by him to the brāhmaṇas and subsequently renewed by his descendant Bhāskaravarman was located formed parts of the dynastic territory.

5. CONTACTS WITH OTHER INDIAN POWERS

We may now take a survey of the contacts Prāgjyotisha had with the ruling powers of the other parts of India. Unfortunately the extant evidence on this point is very meagre and some of it is again beset with uncertainties.

The first in a chronological order and of a purely socio-political nature is the marriage of a Prāgjyotisha princess named Amṛitaprabhā with the Kashmir king Meghavāhana narrated in the *Rāja-taraṅgiṇī* of the celebrated Kashmiri historian Kalhaṇa. He informs us that when king Āryarāja became wholly addicted to quietism and paid no attention to the affairs of the kingdom, his subjects became disaffected and, when on the lookout for an alternative king, they, under the guidance of their ministers, proceeded to Gandhara and brought from there Meghavāhana and got him anointed as king of Kashmir. This prince, as reported by Kalhaṇa, was the great-great-grandson of Yudhishṭhira and son of Gopāditya whom the Gandhara king had detained with the object of using him for vanquishing the king of Kashmir. This prince, prior to being brought to Kashmir for kingship, had, on the advice of his detained father, gone to attend the *svayaṁvara* of the princess Amṛitaprabhā of Prāgjyotisha. Her choice fell on Meghavāhana, and after the latter returned to his father accompanied by his wife, the ministers of Kashmir approached him and brought and installed him as king without any resistance from the reigning king Āryarāja and he was welcomed by all the subjects.[130] Unfortunately, the name of the king of Prāgjyotisha whose daughter Amṛitaprabhā was has not been given by Kalhaṇa, giving rise to uncertainty in the matter. However, M.A. Stein, basing on Kalhaṇa's chronological scheme, has calculated the traditional date for the accession of Meghavāhana which falls in the year 3088 of the Laukika era, the same as the Kali age.[131] Basing on this calculation, D. Sharma feels that this event took place in the first century AD,[132] and to be specific, about AD 56.[133] We must remember, however, that the earlier part of the chronology of Kalhaṇa is wide of the mark by several centuries and that if we were to follow his chronology, we shall have to place Aśoka, Kanishka, Vasishka, Toramāṇa and Mihirakula considerably earlier than has been ascertained on the basis of other dependable considerations.[134] However, Kalhaṇa himself affords evidence to show that Meghavāhana flourished somewhat earlier than Toramāṇa. According to him, Meghavāhana was followed by Śreshṭhisena and the latter by Toramāṇa.[135] Kalhaṇa informs us that this Toramāṇa struck coins in his own name extensively.[136] And in fact, the coins bearing the name of Toramāṇa have been recovered in exceptionally large quantity from several regions including Kashmir. These coins bear his name in Brāhmī characters of about end-fifth century AD.[137] Thus, Meghavāhana also should have flourished about two generations earlier than Toramāṇa. Now, K.L. Barua[138] and, following his lead, some other historians of Kāmarūpa including P.C. Choudhury[139] and M.M. Sharma[140] identify the Prāgjyotisha king whose daughter Amṛitaprabhā is reported to have chosen prince Meghavāhana for her spouse with king Balavarman, grandson of Pushyavarman. However, it is just not possible chronologically for the grandson of a contemporary of the Gupta emperor Samudra Gupta, as Pushyavarman undoubtedly was, to have flourished about mid-fifth century AD. We therefore feel that the Prāgjyotisha monarch in question was most probably Balavarman's great-grandson Mahendravarman who was a very powerful monarch as indicated by his observance of two Aśvamedha sacrifices which probably indicate his bringing the whole of Prāgjyotisha under his political authority or influence. Amṛitaprabhā is reported to have erected a monastery called after her own name Amṛitabhavana for the use of foreign *bhikshus*, and the spiritual guide (*guru*) of her father, who belonged to a foreign country called Loh and was called in the language of his country Stumpā, built the stūpa known as Lo-stonpā.[141] Although all the kings of the line of Pushyavarman were devoted to Śiva and were staunch adherents of Vedic-Paurāṇic systems, they, in keeping with the age-old policy of sectarian toleration, could have patronised Buddhism and Buddhists and paid respect to Buddhist luminaries without adopting Buddhism formally[142] as was the case with Harsha Śilāditya and his contemporary Kāmarūpa king Bhāskaravarman alias Kumāra.[143]

Other documented contacts were of a military nature. Some powers of North India lay claims to success against the Prāgjyotisha kings or reaching the river Lauhitya (Brahmaputra) in course of their military expeditions. Thus, the Mandasor stone pillar inscription of the Aulikara king Yaśodharman Vishṇuvardhana (second quarter of the sixth century AD) speaks of his conquest of the whole area up to the Lauhitya.[144] While there is nothing impossible in an ambitious energetic king of Central India as Yaśodharman undoubtedly was making it to the boundary of Kāmarūpa, it appears more as a conventional claim to victory (*digvijaya*) over the whole of the traditional sphere of the influence of a universal monarch (*chakravarti-kshetra*) than a real conquest in view of the fact that he also stakes claim to reaching the Mahendra mountain, the Himālayas and the western ocean.[145]

The description in the Aphsad inscription of the Later Gupta monarch Ādityasena that the fame of his ancestor Mahāsenagupta due to his astounding victory in war over Susthitavarman was sung on the banks of the river Lauhitya[146] looks more realistic in view of the specificity of the statement. Of course, the nature of the encounter and victory and whether it resulted in the occupation of some territory under Susthitavarman are matters which can not be answered in the absence of any other information.

It is obvious from these and other later allusions[147] that Kāmarūpa was not an isolated area but in frequent communication with the rest of India of which it was culturally an integral part from very early times. The frequent contacts with other parts of the Indian subcontinent contributed to further strengthening this bond.

6. INSTITUTION OF AGRĀHĀRAS AND PATRONAGE OF VEDIC-PAURĀṆIC LEARNING

A very important step in the direction of preserving and strengthening the Vedic-Paurāṇic culture which had already been well-known and popular in Prāgjyotisha and integrating the region with the rest of India much more closely was to settle learned brāhmaṇas and create their settlements. Both the hitherto known records of Bhāskaravarman, the last hitherto known king of the Varman dynasty, viz. Dūbī[148] and Nidhānpur[149] copperplate charters, aim at recording such activities. But they were meant only for the renewal of the two land-grants made by his predecessor Bhūtivarman and are not his own grants. Thus, the Dūbī plates inform us that the copperplate charter in respect of the land alienated to the brāhmaṇas had suffered an all-round damage and therefore Bhāskaravarman gave a charter to the same beneficiaries after brightening it.[150] Likewise, we learn from the Nidhānpur plates that the land granted by Bhūtivarman had become subject to taxes (*kara-da*) because of the loss of the copperplate charter and consequently Bhāskaravarman had to order the preparation of a fresh charter which he handed over to the same brāhmaṇas.[151] The concluding portion of the inscription tells us that after the burning given by him (Bhāskaravarman) the newly written letters looked different from those of the earlier-written grant, but on that account the charter should not be treated as forged.[152] Although we are told in both the cases that Bhāskaravarman re-granted the land to the original donees, it could not have been so, for there was a gap of as many as three generations (and four kings) between the original benefactor (Bhūtivarman) and the re-grantor (Bhāskaravarman). And in most cases the same (or similar) number of generations must have separated the original beneficiaries and those recorded in the two charters. What appears to be meant is that the lands in question were given afresh to the lineal male descendants of the original donees. The number of the donees named in the two grants is quite considerable, viz. at least sixteen in the Dūbī grant[153] and 208 in the Nidhānpur plates.[154] The original number must have been at least thrice, if not more, less than the number recorded in the two charters.[155]

Unfortunately, the Dūbī charter is reticent about the place of issue of the charter as well as the nomenclature and location of the village where the donated land was situated with the result that we are just unable to identify it. But since the charter was found in the Kāmrūp district of Āssām, we may justifiably conclude that the granted land must have been situated somewhere in that district and probably in or near the village of Dūbī which lies about three miles from the Pāṭhshālā railway station.

However, we are more fortunate in this matter in respect of the Nidhānpur plates which supply us full information on these points though it has led to a great debate among scholars. This charter was issued from the *jaya-skandhāvāra* located at Karṇasuvarṇa.[156] The word *skandhāvāra*, whether prefixed by *jaya* or without it, may denote a military camp or capital,[157] but in all probability it (Karṇasuvarṇa) served as the Kāmarūpa capital at the time of the issue of this charter.[158] It has not yet been identified satisfactorily, but was certainly situated somewhere in West Bengal.[159] The original name of the donated village has been read by some as Brahmottara[159a] which was included in the *vishaya* (district) of Chandrapurī and was turned into an *agrāhāra* known as Mayūra-śālmal-āgrāhāra.[160] The points forming its borders included dried up river Kauśikā (east) and the same dry river Kauśikā, marked by hewn fig tree (south-east), Gaṅgiṇikā[160a] together with another hewn fig tree (south-west), Gaṅgaṇikā (west), a potters' pit together with Gaṅgaṇikā (west-north), a large *Jāṭalī* tree (north) and a money-lender's stepped well and the same dried up river Kauśikā (north-east).[161] But despite such a detailed and specific description, there has been much uncertainty about even rough location of the granted village. In this connection P.N. Bhattacharya is inclined to locate the donated village to the west of Kāmarūpa in Puṇḍravardhana-*bhukti*. In this context he invites our attention to the occurrence of the name Gaṅgiṇikā together with a name resembling Mayūra-śālmal-āgrāhāra in the Khalīmpur plate of the Pāla king Dharmapāla.[162] He also points out that the name Gaṅgiṇikā is not in use now in Kāmarūpa but is still in vogue to its west.[163] Our attention is also drawn to the Tezpur grant of Vanamālavarman which records the grant of what is called Abhiśūra-vāṭaka situated to the west of the river Trisrotā (modern Teesta) and a Chandrapuri is spoken of as its south-eastern boundary.[164] But some scholars, not satisfied with this location, propose to place the donated village further west in Bihar. K.L. Barua, for example, thinks that the village in question was situated in the Purneā district of Bihar, for he identifies the river Kauśikā mentioned as one of the boundaries of the donated village with the modern Kosi in Bihar.[165] He is followed by some other scholars including P.C. Choudhury,[166] M.M. Sharma[167] and D. Sharma[168] who have not adduced any additional evidence in its support. However, both these locations (in West Bengal and Bihar) are negated by some well-known facts and historical considerations. First, this notion is, at least partly, inspired by the fact of the charter being given from Karṇasuvarṇa which was certainly to the west of Kāmarūpa. However, it was only the renewed charter that was issued by Bhāskaravarman from his capital at Karṇasuvarṇa which he had wrested from the Gauḍa monarch Śaśāṅka who was his dreaded foe, and it is most unlikely that the original grant of his ancestor Bhūtivarman was also given from this location. We have explicit evidence to show that during the reign of Bhūtivarman and since much prior to it and for a few decades thereafter the region to the immediate west of Kāmarūpa was known as the province (*bhukti*) of Puṇḍravardhaa and formed an integral part of the Gupta empire. As many as five copperplate charters of the later Gupta age have been found at the village of Damodarpur (Dīnājpur district, Bangladesh).[169] All these refer to the Puṇḍravardhana-*bhukti* as being administered by some vassals (*uparika-mahārājas*) on behalf of the imperial Guptas.[170] We are not in the instant case concerned with two of the plates of Kumāra Gupta I's reign dated in the Gupta years 124[171] and 129.[172] But nos. 3 and 4 belong to the reign of Budha Gupta,[173] though their dates are not fully preserved.[174] However, we know from other records of his time that he ruled in *c.* AD 475-95.[175] But the last one (no. 5) belonging to a king the first component of whose name has been damaged[176] is dated in the Gupta year 214[177] which is equivalent to AD 533-34. These inscriptions reveal that continuously from at least Kumāra Gupta I's reign early in the fifth century AD till AD 533-34, if not beyond, the Puṇḍravardhana-*bhukti* was included in the Gupta empire and there could be absolutely no question of its incorporation in the kingdom under Bhūtivarman who, at the latest, reigned in the end-fifth–early sixth century AD. Thus the renewal of the grant by Bhāskaravarman from his capital is of no significance in the present context and it only shows that at the time of the renewal he was in possession of a considerable part of his enemy Śaśāṅka's kingdom, to which we shall advert in the following chapter.

Unless there is anything definitely to prove that the case is otherwise, a charter ought, in the normal course, to be taken to record grant of land in the proximity of its provenance. There are, of course, exceptions,[178] but they only serve to prove the rule. And this is naturally the view of most of the scholars who have cared to work on this inscription. J.C. Ghosh locates the granted land in Pañchakhaṇḍa region of the Sylhet (ancient Śrīhaṭṭa) district in modern Bangladesh where the plates were found.[179] He has demonstrated that all the now recognisable boundaries are present in the Pañchakhaṇḍa region. Thus all the rivers are called Gaṅg in East Bengal (present Bangladesh) and it is a short or colloquial form of Gaṅgā and Gaṅgiṇikā is Gaṅg's Sanskritised form for a rivulet. Then Kauśikā can easily be equated with the present river Kusiara flowing by the north-west of Panchakhanda. There is a place called Chandrapur or Chandapura near the present village of Bagasurā. There could have been and were in actuality different towns of the same name in different regions, and we can not insist that

Chandrapuri-*vishaya* mentioned in the charter in question is necessarily identical with Chandrapari corrected to Chandrapurī located to the west of the river Trisrotā as done by P.N. Bhattacharya. Moreover, as pointed out by K.K. Gupta, the Paśchimbāg copperplate of king Śrīchandra of *circa* tenth century AD refers to a Chandrapura-*vishaya* situated within the Śrīhaṭṭa-*maṇḍala* which was included within the Puṇḍravardhana-*bhukti*.[180] It is not unlikely that the Sylhet region was not originally included in the Puṇḍravardhana-*bhukti* during the time of Bhūtivarman but came to be incorporated within this *bhukti* under later administrative regroupings. This view about the location of the land alienated by Bhūtivarman as known from his descendant's Nidhānpur charter is also shared by several other authorities incuding P.L. Paul,[181] Amarnath Ray,[182] K.M. Gupta,[183] D.R. Bhandarkar[184] and N.K. Bhattasali[185] as well as others.[186]

The provenance of the Nidhānpur charter and the location of the land granted by Bhūtivarman through it and the find-spot of his only known record, viz. Baḍagaṅgā rock inscription, in the Nowgong district of Assam would show that he had expanded his kingdom at the cost of Ḍavāka and extended it to the Surma valley (Sylhet region) in present Bangladesh. It is not impossible that it was achieved earlier during the reign of his grandfather Mahendravarman who had observed a couple of horse-sacrifices to signify his military successes. We have some evidence in the Chinese sources indicating, perhaps, that till at least AD 428 Ḍavāka continued to maintain its own political identity. We learn from the account of Thien-chu (India) by Ma-twa-lin that in the fifth year of the Yuen-kia period in the reign of Wen-ti belonging to the Song dynasty in AD 428 king Yuei-'ai (='loved by the moon')[188] of Kia-pi-li (Kapila) in Thien-chu (India) sent an ambassador to present a letter to the emperor and to offer him a ring set with diamonds, a bracelet of pure gold and some other valuable articles together with two parrots, one red and the other white.[187] While we find only the name of the river and not that of the kingdom which is rather strange, the fact that Ḍavāka was situated in the valley of the river Kapilī should leave no doubt that this is the kingdom intended. And the king can not be identified as we know nothing absolutely about the annals of this kingdom. There is, however, no doubt that this small territory as well as the valley of the river Surma where the Sylhet region is situated already formed an integral part of the growing Varman kingdom, thanks to the expansionist policy of its members, more particularly that of Mahendravarman and Bhūtivarman.

An analysis of the **names of the brāhmaṇa beneficiaries** of these two grants is of immense interest to a serious student of the cultural history of Prāgjyotisha. Practically all the donees of the Dūbī plates had *ghosha*-ending names to which the brāhmaṇa honorific *bhaṭṭa* was prefixed and the word *svāmin*, which, too, served as end-honorific, was suffixed. The Nidhānpur charter affords many times more names which provide much more material for an interesting and enlightening study of personal names and cultural history of the region. The allottees of the grant had names terminating in, *inter alia*, *ghosha*, *vasu*, *datta*, *sena*, *kuṇḍa*,[189] *nāga*, *dāma*, *soma*, *bhūti*, *nandin*, *gaṇa*,[190] *mitra*, *dhara*,[191] *rāta*, *dāsa*, etc. Most of them had the word *svāmin* suffixed to their names. From this we may infer justifiably that it was employed as an honorific at the end of the names like *jī* in Hindi, Marathi and Gujarati in our own times. A few of them had for their Veda Bahvṛicha (*Ṛigveda*) and Chhandoga (*Sāmaveda*) while most of the grantees belonged to various recensions (*śākhās*) of the *Yajurveda* including Taittirīya and Charaka in exceptional instances while most of them belonged to the Vājasaneyī *saṁhitā*. They had for their *gotras* Prāchetasa, Kātyāyana, Yāska, Bhāradvāja, Kāśyapa, Kautsa, Gaurātreya, Kṛishṇātreya, Kauṇḍinya, Gautama, Vātsa, Maudgalya, Śaubhaka (or Śaunaka), Pārāśarya, Āśvalāyana, Vārāha, Vaishṇavṛiddhi, Kauśikā, Kauṭilya, Kavestara, Māṇḍavya, Vasishṭha, Agniveśya, Sāṅkṛityāyana, Jātūkarṇa, Pautrimāshya, Paurṇa, Sāvarṇika, Śālaṅkāyana, Gārgya, Ālambāyana, Āṅgirasa, Pāṅkalya, Bārhaspatya, Śaunaka, Vārāha and Śākaṭāyana. What is most astonishing is the fact that most of these originally brāhmaṇa name-endings are now used as popular surnames by the members of the Kāyastha and other lower communities, except *deva*[192] which is met with among the brāhmaṇas. What is even stranger is that these are current only in Bengal (both West Bengal and Bangladesh) and not in Prāgjyotisha.

This strange phenomenon certainly calls for an explanation. It has been shown by Bhandarkar D.R.[193] that these were Nāgara brāhmaṇas who migrated from Nāgarkoṭ in the Uttarāpatha division of Bhāratavarsha (presently in Pakistan) to Kannauj and Mithilā on the one hand and the Valabhī region of Gujarat on the other about the same period, viz. fifth century AD. And it was from Mithilā and Kannauj that they came over to Prāgjyotisha. The story of the Nāgara brāhmaṇas is narrated in the Nāgara-khaṇḍa of the *Skanda-purāṇa* where most of these surnames are met with. It is noteworthy that many of these surnames are encountered among the brāhmaṇa beneficiaries of the Tipperāh grant of king Lokanātha, dated in his 44th regnal year.[194] It is also averred in the Nāgara-khaṇḍa that Hāṭakeśvara Śiva was the *kula-devatā* (tutelary divinity) of the Nāgara brāhmaṇas. It is not impossible that the temple of god Hāṭakeśvara renovated by king Vanamālavarman as per his Tezpur grant[195] was originally built by the Nāgara brāhmaṇas during the reign of Bhūtivarman. It is pertinent to note in the present context that seven shares of the land granted by him through the Nidhānpur charter were allotted for the offerings (*bali* and *charu*) to the god and for the charitable feeding house (*sattra*), evidently attached to a temple,[196] which not impossibly might have been of Hāṭakeśvara, as surmised by some.

Scholars have attempted various explanations of this curious feature concerning the surnames. It has, for instance, been suggested that these indicate the intermixture with the Alpines, the Nāgara brāhmaṇas and Kāyasthas.[197] But we feel that this feature can be easily explained away by assuming that originally Kāyastha was a professional, not caste, designation and several brāhmaṇas could have held this office. But later when the profession became hereditary and its followers turned into a caste (*jāti*), the surnames used by them earlier turned into caste surnames of the Kāyasthas. And because they had become surnames of the members of this newly formed caste, traditional brāhmaṇas deliberately eschewed them.

The donated land is said to have been converted into what is called an ***agrahāra*** known as Mayūra-śālmal-āgrāhāra-kshetra.[198] In most other inscriptions also the term is spelt as *agrahāra* with no medial sign for *ā* (*dīrgha ā*) in its second component (*gra*), and there has naturally been considerable uncertainty about its exact connotation. According to D.C. Sircar, it denotes 'rent-free land given to Brāhmaṇas, a rent-free village, a Brāhmaṇa village; sometimes suffixed to names of localities especially in South India'. It was primarily, 'a rent-free village in the possession of the Brāhmaṇas'.[199] He also notices the expressions *dev-āgrāhāra* (rent-free village in possession of a deity), *Vaiśy-āgrāhāra* (rent-free holding in the possession of the Vaiśyas), *Agrahārika*, *Āgrahārika*, *Agrahārn*, etc.[200] Though he notices the form of the word *agrāhāra* also occurring in some epigraphs, he is unable to determine as to which form is the correct one, though he appears to regard the form with the second component without the indication of the length of *a* (viz. ā) as preferable.[201] Most other scholars have also adopted the same form. But *agrahāra* does not yield a good or satisfactory meaning. The correct form is with the length of *a* in the second syllable of the word which ought to be ***agrāhāra***, and fortunately this form is employed consistently in the copperplate grants of the Mahārājas of Valkha and those of the Parivrājaka Mahārājas of the Baghelkhand region of Central India.[202] Thus, in several charters of the former we find that the land granted to the divinities and brāhmaṇas is called *agrāhāra*,[203] and the same is the case with the grants of the Parivrājaka Mahārājas.[204] And this form affords an excellent meaning, viz. food (or maintenance) of the foremost people (*agra* =foremost, chief; *āhāra* = food, subsistence). The most consistent evidence in this respect is, however, afforded by the inscriptions of the Mahārājas of Valkha which contain not only the word *agrāhāra* but also numerous allied formations like *agrāhāra-ny*āya,[205] *brahmadey-āgrāhāra-bhukti*,[206] *brahmadeya-kul-āgrāhāra-nyāya*,[207] *chāturvaidy-āgrāhāra*.[208] *dev-āgrāhāra*,[209] *dev-āgrāhāra-bhukti*,[210] *dev-āgrāhāraka*,[211] *dev-āgrāhāra-krama*,[212] *dev-āgrāhāra-nyāya*,[213] *ṛitvig-āgrāhāraka*[214] and *yajñāgrāhāraka*.[215] Such a rich crop of consistently spelt references leaves no doubt that the correct and meaningful form of the word is *agrāhāra* and not *agrahāra*. Accordingly, the altered name of the alienated Brāhmaṇa village should only have been Mayūra-śālmal-āgrāhāra. And if the name is meaningful as it may be expected justifiably, it and its proximity must have abounded in the peacocks and silk-cotton trees. And it is almost certain that such a large brāhmaṇa settlement must have contributed substantially to the promotion of Vedic and other religious and secular learning and popular education in the region.

NOTES AND REFERENCES

1. *Indian Archaeology 1956-57: A Review*, p. 82.
2. For a gist of these reports, see A.K. Sharma, *Emergence of Early Culture in North-East India (A Study based on Excavation at Bhaitbari, Meghalaya)*, pp. 12-13.
3. For a detailed illustrated account, *vide ibid.*, pp. 24-30.
4. *Vide ibid.*, pp. 31-35
5. For a detailed account, see *ibid.*, pp. 36-42. We do not find it possible to agree with the author in his description of the Śiva temple as an Ashṭamūrti one containing eight Śiva-liṅgas (pp. 38 and 42), for the term *ashṭa-mūrti* has nothing to do with the number of the *liṅgas* but refers just to a Śiva image with eight faces such as the one described by Kālidāsa in the inaugural versified invocation in his play *Abhijñāna-Śākuntala* and visibly illustrated by an exquisite eight-faced Śiva figure from Mandhal (Nagpur district, Maharashtra) dating from early Vākāṭaka phase (early fourth century AD) and presently deposited in the Central Museum at Nāgpur.
6. Largest numerically, the Gaṇeśa figures were apparently most popular in the region as at present.
7. It is erroneously described as Brahmā by Sharma (p. 50 and the caption of pl. XXXII) whereas the three eyes (two normal, and the third above them in the centre) should leave no doubt whatsoever about it being a Śiva figure, for the third eye is one of the iconographic attributes of god Śiva. Indra, too, has this mark, but in the absence of other distinguishing features, he is out of picture in the instant case.

7a. Sharma has taken these figures as of male musicians playing on the lyre calling them Vīṇādharas. But even a casual look at them is enough to convince anyone that they are female figures and their representation as playing on *vīṇā* is proof enough that these are in fact figures of goddess Sarasvatī.

8. The author has mentioned an ascetic pregnant woman (p. 62 and caption of pl. XII), but asceticism and pregnancy are simply contradictory and consequently an unimaginable concept. Moreover, the figure has no feminine characteristics.

8a. These have been called Gandharva by Sharma, but the absence of any musical instrument in their hands and the presence of the garland appears to suggest Vidyādhara figures.

9. The figure at pl. XLIX does not look female and there appears to be a moustache which evidences its male character.
10. This is the only charter to contain this statement whereas the remainder of the description beginning with Naraka and legends concerning him are reiterated in most other charters belonging to several other dynasties ruling over the region one after the other.
11. For a detailed discussion of this point and supporting evidence, *vide* his *KŚ*, pp. 36-37 and 93-96.
12. *EHK*, p. 41. He just felt that the name of the Kāmarūpa king Pushyavarman was probably given after the renowned Śuṅga king Pushyamitra of Magadha

just as Pushyavarman's son and successor Samudravarman was named after Samudra Gupta, the celebrated Gupta emperor.

13. The expression in the original is *Naṁdarāja-ti-vasa-sata*, which has been taken to mean erroneously 103 years which is quite inconsistent with several other hypotheses of the scholars dating Khāravela's reign in the early second century BC and regarding him as a contemporary of the Śuṅga king Pushyamitra.

14. Sharma (*KŚ*, pp. 94-95), who doubts the inscriptional evidence in this regard, has not himself been able to cut much ice. That the inscriptions do not name Pushyavarman's chief queen as in the other succeeding cases, that he was an upstart whose whereabouts before he became a king were unknown, and that the panegyrists were cut off from the real tradition, though quite interesting, are far from convincing to prove his contention. However, the fact that both the composers of the two *praśastis* and the seal-inscriptions do not mention Pushyavarman's chief queen may perhaps indicate that he was just an upstart for, as will be shown in the sequence, he was the (or a) son of an ordinary personage named Naraka after the dynasty's traditional homonymous progenitor.

15. Surendravarman known from the Umāchal rock inscription of his reign (*IAA*, p. 2), which is as yet the earliest known epigraph from Prāgjyotisha, was definitely not the same as king Mahendravarman as conjectured by some scholars. It does not prove, however, that the drafters of the official charters and the legends on the two hitherto known seals were unaware of the true position and that there was some gap between Pushyavarman and his (alleged, according to Sharma) son and successor Samudravarman. We also are of the opinion that the suggested identity of Surendravarman of the Umāchal rock inscription and Mahendravarman, son and successor of Gaṇapativarman, is totally unwarranted. But we feel that he was a collateral member (or a rebel holding authority over some region concurrently with some other member of the family) and as he was not followed on the throne by his son, he was not in direct line and as such found no place in the family tree as in several other cases. But the non-mention of Pushyavarman's chief queen as against all of his descendants in the official records is not totally bereft of historical significance and may suggest that he was not an important king and, as we shall show presently, he was the (or a) son of an ordinary personage called Naraka.

16. *Vide* M. Pauthier, 'Thien-chu - India: Extract from Ma-twa-lin, Book CCCXXXVIII. Fol. 14', *IA*, 1880, pp. 14-15. See also P.C. Bagchi, *India and China*, pp. 7f., 16f.; Motichandra, *Trade and Trade Routes in Ancient India*, p. 2.

17. For the English rendering of the work and discussion on it, see J.W. McCrindle, *Ancient India as Described in the Classical Literature*; W.H. Schoff, *The Periplus of the Erythrean Sea*; 'Anonymi (Ut Fertur) Periplus Maris Erythraei', *IA*, VIII, 1879, pp. 107-51; R.C. Majumdar (ed.), *Classical Accounts of India*. The references and citations in these pages, unless otherwise specified, are from the last-named work.

18. For the latest detailed account of various theories on the question and

support for the latter half of the first century AD date, *vide* Joe Cribb, 'Numismatic Evidence for the Date of the "Periplus" ', *Numismatics, History, Art & Culture: Essays in Honour of Dr. Parmeshwari Lal Gupta*, pp. 121-37; Ajay Mitra Shastri, *The Sātavāhanas and the Western Kshatrapas: A Historical Framework*, pp. 138-39, 141, note 5.

19. The Kirrhadae are described as 'savages whose noses are flattened to the face'. *Vide CAI*, p. 307.
20. The areas identified by scholars as south-east Bengal and Sylhet are presently included in Bangladesh.
21. Masalia, despite different speculative conjectures, may now be identified fairly definitely with the coastal region of Andhra Pradesh anciently known as Māhishaka in the light of the recently discovered evidence in the form of its mention along with Kaliṅga in the Guṇṭupalli quadruple pillar inscriptions.
22. These tribes included, in addition to the Kirrhadae, Bargysoi, Hippioprosopoi, also known as Makroprosopoi, who are said to have been horse-faced or long-faced and were reported to have been cannibals. *Vide ibid.*, pp. 307-8.
23. The notions of the classical authors about the easternmost regions were still far from clear.
24. See *ibid.*, pp. 307-8, for the *Periplus* description of the Chryse country. Pliny's location of this region as well as of Argyre as beyond the mouth of the Indus (*ibid.*, p. 345) appears to be wide of the mark and does not tally with other classical writers.
25. *JASB*, 1847, I, pp. 20-27.
26. *Commerce and Navigation of the Erythrean Sea*, pp. 145-49.
27. Schoff, *Periplus*, Introduction, pp. 10 and 55.
28. *Vide HCPA*, p. 31.
29. *Vide CAI*, p. 308.
30. See *IAA*, p. 96, verse 1.
31. *Ibid.*, p. 116, verse 1.
32. *Fathiya-i-Ibriyah* informs us that some ten thousand people were occupied in gold-washings, each one of them making on an average one *tolā* of gold per year and handing it over to the king. Under the Ahoms also large-scale gold-washing was practised by the gold-washers called *Sonovāls* and the state levied an annual tax from them. See *CHA*, p. 95 and notes.
33. Schoff, *op. cit.*, pp. 47-48, 261, 278; McCrindle, *Commerce and Navigation of the Periplus*, pp. 145ff.
34. The description of the festival runs as follows (*CAI*, pp. 308-9): On the confines, however, of Thinai an annual fair is held, attended by a race of men of squat figure, with their face very flat, but mild in disposition, called the Sesatai, who (in appearance resemble wild animals). They come with their wives and children to the fair, bringing heavy loads of goods wrapped up in mats resembling in outward appearance the early leaves of vine. Their place of assembly is where their own territory borders on that of Thinai; and here, squatted on the mats on which they exhibit their wares, they feast for several days, after which they return to their homes in the interior. On observing

their retreat the people of Thinai, repairing to the spot, collect the mats on which they had been sitting, and taking out the fibres, which are called *petroi*, from the reeds, they put the leaves two and two together and roll them up into slender balls, through which they pass the fibres extracted from the reeds.

35. For references, see *ibid.*, p. 308.
36. Both McCrindle (*Commerce and Navigation*, pp. 145ff.) and Whiteley (*The Periplus*, Introduction, pp. 10, 567ff.) locate Thina or This in the western part of China, though the former locates the Sesatai in the proximity of Sylheṭ now forming part of Bangladesh.
37. J.W. McCrindle, *Ancient India as described in Classical Literature*, p. 26.
38. *Ibid.*, fn. 2.
39. *Ibid.*, p. 178. There appears to have been some confusion in Greek sources and McCrindle thinks that Alexander did not make his way to the Ganges but penetrated to Serica where the people called Seres produced silk. But, as will be seen from other references in classical literature, Seres inhabited the North-East earlier included in Assam.
40. *CAI*, pp. 346-47.
41. The Roman traders deposited the wares they brought for sale to the Seres, who removed them if satisfied and left their own wares in return on the further bank of a river in their own country. See *ibid.*
42. Though the work was composed around AD 150, Ptolemy had started collecting material for it several decades earlier.
43. He calls its capital Sera. *Vide CAI*, p. 356.
44. *JASB*, 1847, pp. 43ff.
45. For some plausible suggestions about the identification of these rivers and of certain other regions and localities mentioned by some classical writers with those in the North-East, *vide HCPA*, pp. 33-38 and 95-96.
46. *Vide KŚ*, pp. 95-96.
47. Cited by B.K. Barua in his *CHA*, p. 16. According to Kakati, Naraka of Mithilā (viz. Videha) with its capital at Mithilā was a political adventurist who established himself in power in Prāgjyotisha somewhere during this period. B.K. Barua refrains from giving his own view, but he obviously agreed with Kakati.
48. As we shall see shortly, Pushyavarman could not have lived later than about the beginning of the second quarter of the fourth century AD.
49. *HCPA*, pp. 124-25. He compares Naraka to the demon Bāṇa both of whom were historical personages, the former's historicity being established by the presence of the village called Narakāsuragāon near Guwahati and the latter's by that of Agnigaḍh, Agni-parvata and other localities in the neighbourhood of Tezpur.
50. He adds some more rulers to the list of the Varman kings beginning with Pushyavarman whom they preceded and the total of the two groups of kings claiming their descent from Naraka, numbering 24 or 26, ruled for a period of about 600 years allowing an average of twenty-five years to each reign. Assuming that Pushyavarman flourished around mid-fourth century AD

and allowing another 300 years to the predecessors, he places Naraka and Bhagadatta about the first century AD. Naraka and Bhagadatta are consequently taken by him as dynastic titles. *Vide ibid.*, p. 132.

51. After Bhūmi (earth) who was their traditional female progenitor.
52. After the Boar (Varāha) incarnation of Vishṇu who was believed to be their male progenitor.
53. Because Naraka happened to be their first royal ancestor.
54. This nomenclature owes itself to their name-ending *varman*.
55. *IAA*, pp. 11ff. ; *KŚ*, Part II, pp. 8ff.
56. *Ibid.*, pp. 20ff.; *IAA*, pp. 40ff.
57. Both these charters were originally issued by Bhūtivarman and when it was found that they had become unavailable for certain reasons they had to be re-issued by Bhāskaravarman. But the genuineness of these charters appears suspect, and we intend to discuss this problem in detail elsewhere.
58. *IAA*, p. 33; *KŚ*, Part II, pp. 17-18.
59. Hirananda Sastri, *Nālandā and its Epigraphical Material*, *Memoirs of the Archaeological Survey of India*, No. 66, 1942, pp. 69-70. Two seals of Bhāskaravarman were found in the ruins of Nālandā, and both were of reddish baked clay. Of the first only a portion of the left lower side was recovered, and the second was found in two parts which, when joined together, give us almost the full seal with the text and the device complete in all respects. These seals were evidently affixed to some letters or goods sent by the Prāgjyotisha emperor to some monastic chief at the provenance. They might have been brought by the two messengers of Bhāskaravarman for sealing their own communications on their patron's behalf.
60. *Bhagadatta-Vajradatt- ānvayo* is the expression in the original.
61. *Harsha-charita*, p. 295.
62. 'Aśvamedhas celebrated by Kāmarūpa Kings', *IHQ*, XXI, 1945, p. 144; 'Note on Baḍagaṅgā Inscription of Bhūtivarman', *EI*, XXX, 1953-54, p. 65 (the entire expression *Naraka-tanayo Bhagadatta-Vajradatt-ānvayo* is here rendered as 'descendant of Naraka as well as of Bhagadatta and Vajradatta'); his inconvenience is transparent enough in his observation on the point, viz. 'The use of the word *tanaya* in the secondary sense of "a male descendant" in preference to its primary sense of "a son", especially in view of the word *anvaya* used in the adjoining expression, is rather peculiar.' See *IHQ*, XXI, 1945, p. 144.
63. *IAA*, p. 35.
64. *KŚ*, Part III, p. 160.
65. This goes well with D. Sharma's above-cited suggestion about the existence of more than one personage named Naraka, but the age for these three Narakas propounded by him is considerably earlier. But that emboldens us in our instant theory.
66. *Vide* Hirananda Sastri, *op. cit.* , Pl. IX (a-b), line 1.
67. 'Dūbī Plates of Bhāskaravarman', *EI*, XXX, 1953-54, p. 288, line 1. The illustration of the seal opposite p. 305 is not clear enough to ascertain the correct reading, but as Sircar was an accomplished epigraphist, his reading

need not be doubted much.

68. A photograph of the seal supplied kindly by Dr M.D. Sampath, Director (Epigraphy), Archaeological Survey of India, Mysore, also was not found useful for this purpose as the relevant portion in this photograph also is quite faint.

68a. For a full discussion of this problem, see Ajay Mitra Shastri, 'New Light on the Ancient History of Prāgjyotisha: Pushyavarman was son of Naraka', *JARS*, XXXV, 1995, pp. 32-35.

69. While this is the genealogy and order of succession supported by all the extant sources, different sources reveal some minor variations in regard to the spellings of personal names. Thus, the name of the queen of Samudravarman is given as Dattavatī in the Nālandā seals and the Dūbī plates as against Dattadevī met with in Dūbī seal and the Nidhānpur plates; that of Balavarman's queen figures as Ratnadevī in the Dūbī plates as opposed to Ratnavatī found elsewhere; Nārāyaṇavarman's queen is called Devamatī in the Dūbī and Nālandā seals instead of Devavatī in other sources; while the spelling Bhūtivarman is vouched for by his own Baḍagaṅgā rock inscription, the Nālandā and Dūbī seals and Bāṇabhaṭṭa's *Harsha-charita*, the Dūbī and Nidhānpur charters prefix the name with the word *mahat* (viz. the name is given as Mahābhūtivarman); Sthitavarman is mentioned as Sthitivarman by Bāṇa and as Sthiravarman in the Nālandā seals, while his queen is called Nayanaśobhā in the Nālandā seals; his son's name is found spelt as Susthiravarman by Bāṇa and on the seals from Nālandā, and that of his *mahādevī* as Śyāmalakshmī on the Nālandā seals and Dhruvalakshmī on the Dūbī seal.

70. *IAA*, pp. 17-18, verses 62ff.

71. *Ibid.*, p. 42, verses 20-21.

72. The imperial style is not applied to any of the rulers in the Dūbī and Nidhānpur charters of Bhāskaravarman as they are metrical and it was not expedient to use any regal title in verses.

73. All the seal-inscriptions mentioning this title belong to his reign.

74. This style had lost its original significance by this time and is known to have been employed at least sometimes even for feudal chiefs.

75. *Harsha-charita*, p. 295.

75a. For a discussion, see Ajay Mitra Shastri, 'Seals and Sealings of Bhāskaravaman, King of Prāgjyotisha', *Studies in Indian Epigraphy*, XXVI, 2000, pp. 20-34.

76. The north-eastern portion of the Kāmākhyā hill is known as Nīlāchal or Umāchal, and the record in question was found engraved on its north-eastern slope.

77. *Vide* D.C. Sircar and P.D. Choudhury, 'Umachal Rock Inscription of Surendravarman', *EI*, XXXI, 1955-56, pp. 67-69.

78. *Ibid.*, p. 69, lines 2-3. Here Baladeva is called Balabhadra-svāmin.

79. *Ibid.*, p. 68. This identification, which was 'tentative', was based also on the fact that this short inscription is datable on palaeographical grounds slightly earlier than Bhūtivarman's Baḍagaṅgā inscription.

80. Bāṇa mentions only his march against the Gauḍa king and ends with the recovery of his sister Rājyaśrī who had fled to the forest due to calamities unleashed by Śaśāṅka.

81. For a discussion on the date of the *Harsha-charita*, see S.R. Goyal, *Harsha and Buddhism*, pp. 143-49. Some others had also proposed this date for the composition of the work, but without proper evidence. A.B. Keith, however, argues for a date in the later years of Harshavardhana's reign, but his arguments do not carry conviction.

82. K.L. Barua (*EHK*, p. 54) stresses the point that in Harsha's assembly at Kannauj in AD 644 Bhāskaravarman played the role of Brahmā and Harsha that of Indra which, according to him, indicates that the former was older than the latter. In view of it he dates Bhāskaravarman's accession about AD 600.

83. Naraka, the father of Pushyavarman, who as shown above, is mentioned in all the seal-inscriptions, was an ordinary personage without pretension to regal authority.

84. Some scholars like K.L. Barua (*ibid.*, p. 54) give 20 years to a generation and accordingly date the rise of Pushyavarman to power around AD 380. It must be noted, however, that when Barua wrote Surendravarman and Supratishṭhitavarman were not known. However, following the period allotted by him as per rule, this event might date around AD 340.

85. Various dates have been proposed for Pushyavarman's rise to power. N.N. Vasu (*Social History of Kāmarūpa*, I, p. 141) dates Pushyavarman's reign in *c.* AD 275-300. Other scholars place it somewhat later at different dates in the fourth century AD. R.C. Majumdar (*HCIP*, III: *CA*, p. 89) dates Pushyavarman's accession about AD 350 or a little earlier, while D.C. Sircar and P.D. Chaudhury (*EI*, XXXI, 1955-56, p. 68) are inclined to place his reign in *circa* AD 350-74). This dating was, however, influenced at least to some extent by the erroneous notion that the Baḍgaṅgā inscription contained a date in the Gupta era which Sircar himself found baseless on a personal examination of the record later. But we feel it better to remain open regarding this question in the absence of a definitive evidence and place his accession early in the fourth century AD, most probably in the beginning of the second quarter of this century.

86. The bordering powers also included some republican people like the Mālavas, Ārjunāyanas, Yaudheyas, Mādrakas, Ābhīras, Prārjūnas, Sanakānīkas, Kākas and Kharaparikas.

87. *Samataṭa-Ḍavāka-Kāmarūpa-Nepāla-Kartṛipur-ādi-pratyanta-nṛipatibhir....sarvva-kara-dān-ājñā-karaṇa-praṇām-āgamana-paritoshita-prachaṇḍa-śāsanasya.*

D.R. Bhandarkar (Revisor), B. Ch. Chhabra and G.S. Gai (editors), *Inscriptions of the Early Gupta Kings*, *CII*, III, p. 213, lines 22-23.

88. *Early History of India*, pp. 271 and 316.

89. *History of Ancient India*, p. 244.

90. *Researches on Ptolemy's Geography*, pp. 52ff., cited in *HCPA*, p. 145.

91. However, the eras were not always deliberately instituted but resulted more often from the continuation of the regnal reckoning of a king by his successors.

92. Bhandarkar, Chhabra and Gai, *op. cit.*, p. 240, line 3.
93. *Early History of India*, 2nd edn., p. 266; *Imperial Gazetteer*, History, II, p. 290.
94. *Coinage of the Gupta Empire*, p. 2.
95. *Catalogue of the Coins of the Gupta Dynasties and of Śaśāṅka, King of Gauḍa*, Introduction, p. xx. For the view that the era resulted from the continuation of the regnal years of Chandra Gupta I, see J.F. Fleet, *Inscriptions of the Early Gupta Kings and their Successors, CII*, III, Introduction, p. 38, fn. 5.
96. S.R. Goyal, *A History of the Imperial Guptas*, pp. 107-10; *Gupta Sāmrājya kā Itihāsa* (Hindi), p. 10. R.C. Majumdar (*HCIP*, III: *CA*, pp. 4-5) also holds that Samudra Gupta came to power in AD 340 or 350 if he was not the founder of the Gupta era. The same position is reiterated in *A Comprehensive History of India*, III (I), p. 37 where only AD 350 is mentioned as the approximate date for his accession provided, of course, that he was not the initiator of the Gupta era.
97. P.L. Gupta, *Gupta Sāmrājya* (Hindi), p. 277.
98. *Vide* Ajay Mitra Shastri, 'Samudra Gupta's Aśvamedhas', *The Quarterly Journal of the Mythic Society*, LXXXVIII, Part III, July-September 1997, pp. 31-36.
99. For strong arguments in support of this view, see R.C. Majumdar, *A New History of the Indian People*, VI: *The Vākāṭaka-Gupta Age*, pp. 131-32, 158-60; *CA*, pp. 4-5, 16; *A Comprehensive History of India*, III, Part I, pp. 15-16, 35-37.

100. D.C. Sircar in *Bhāratavarsha* (Bengali monthly), 1348 Bengali saṁvat, Part II, p. 397; 1349, Part II, pp. 193 and 262. Cited by R.C. Majumdar in *A Comprehensive History of India*, III, Part I, p. 36, fn. 51. See also D.C. Sircar, *Select Inscriptions bearing on Indian History and Civilization*, I, p. 270, fn. 4.
101. *History of North-Eastern India*, p. 211.
102. *Dynastic History of Northern India*, I, p. 238.
103. *Social History of Kāmarūpa*, I, p. 141.
104. *Proceedings and Transactions of the First All-India Oriental Conference, Summaries of Papers*, 1920, p. cxxiv.
105. 'New Light on the History of Assam', *IHQ*, XXI, 1945, p. 22; 'Baḍagaṅgā Rock Inscription of Bhūtivarman', *EI*, XXVII, 1947-48, pp. 18ff. Unfortunately he read the non-existent year 200 (+) 30 (+) 4 (=234) which he attributed to the Gupta era, thereby taking this inscription as dated in Gupta year 234 which had vitiated his chronology seriously. However, as shown by D.C. Sircar ('Note on the Baḍagaṅgā Inscription of Bhūtivarman', *EI*, XXX, 1953-54, p. 64), no such date is recorded in the inscription and it resulted from his doctored estampage. Earlier Sircar also was misled into accepting it (*IHQ*, XXI, 1945, p. 145: but he preferred to read it as 240) and it was only when he himself personally examined the original stone and had an impression prepared that he realised the error and brought it to scholarly notice.
106. *A List of the Inscriptions of Northern India in Brāhmī and its Derivative Scripts, from about 200 A. C.*, Appendix to *EI*, XIX-XXII, p. 401, fn. 1.
107. N.K. Bhattasali ('New Light on the History of Assam', *IHQ*, XXI, 1945, p. 22), however, feels that Pushyavarman was a contemporary of Chandra Gupta

I and named his son and daughter-in-law after those of his Gupta friend, Chandra Gupta I. However, his view was at least partly due to his wrong chronology based on his reading of the Gupta era date in the Baḍagaṅgā rock inscription of Bhūtivarman.

108. *EHK*, pp. 42-43.
109. See P.C. Choudhury, *HCPA*, p. 145.
110. The Mathura pillar inscription of the time of Chandra Gupta II refers to the Gupta year 61 (= AD 380) as falling in the fifth year of his reign and he was preceded on the throne by his elder brother Rāma Gupta who may have ruled for some five years. Therefore the end of his father Samudra Gupta's reign may be placed roughly around AD 370.
111. The queen of Samudravarman, who must have borne another name given to her by her parents, was obviously renamed after her marriage and now called after the chief queen of her husband's father's patron.
112. We have another parallel instance of a grateful ruler naming his son and successor after his benefactor, viz. the Gaṅga king Ayyavarman naming his son as Mādhava-Siṁhavarman after the Pallava king Siṁhavarman who had installed him on the throne.
113. *HCIP*, III: *CA*, p. 89.
114. This would go well with the imperial title *mahārājādhirāja* applied to him in Bhāskaravarman's records; it is not certain though that he actually himself bore this style. It is not impossible that it was applied to him during the time of Bhāskaravarman when the family had really attained an imperial status.
115. N.K.Bhattasali ('New Light on the History of Assam', *IHQ*, XXI, 1945, pp. 24) observes: 'By the term Pushyamitra, upon which there appears to be a pun (*ślesha*), we should understand the descendants of Pushyavarman of Assam who had so long been *mitras* or friends of the Guptas, but had changed into foes by their *vijigīshā* or desire for conquest, and had invaded the Gupta empire from the east and made it totter.'
116. J.F. Fleet, *CII*, III, p. 54, line 11.
117. *Ibid.*
118. This reading was originally proposed by H.R. Divekar and later adopted by D.R. Bhandarkar (*Inscriptions of the Early Gupta Kings, CII,* III, p. 54), B. Ch. Chhabra ('Beauties of the Bhītarī Inscription of Skandagupta', *Dr. Mirashi Felicitation Volume*, pp. 366ff.) and V.V. Mirashi.
119. F.E. Pargiter, *The Purāṇa Text of the Dynasties of the Kali Age*, p. 51. In addition to the Pushyamitras whose jurisdiction of government is left unspecified, thirteen kings belonging to a ruling family called Paṭumitra (there are numerous but minor variants of the two names in various manuscripts) are mentioned as ruling at Mekalā, the capital of the Maikal country. We feel that the correct reading in all these cases ought to be *Pushyamitra*, not *Paṭumitra* or any such other name. A *kula* of the Vāraṇa *gaṇa* of the Jainas of this name is also known from a Mathurā inscription as pointed out by A.M.T. Jackson (*Bombay Gazetteer*, I, Part i, p. 69, fn. 4).
120. *IAA*, p. 33, lines 6 and 7-8.
121. *Ibid.*, p. 35, lines 4-5 and 7.

122. *Ibid.*, p. 5, line 2: the expression for describing Bhūtivarman as performer of Aśvamedha is *aśvamedha-yājin.* Whether it refers to just one or more Aśvamedhas is a point that can not be ascertained in the present state of insufficient evidence.

123. The relevant expressions in the seal-inscriptions are *śrī-Yajñavatyāṁ śrī-Mahendro dvis = turagamedh-āharttā* (Dūbī seal, lines 5-6) and *śrī-Yajñavatyāṁ śrī-Mahendravarmmā dvis = turagamedh-āharttā* (Nālandā seal, lines 4-5) with reference to Mahendravarman and *śrī-Bhogavatyāṁ dviraśvamedha-yājī śrī-Sthiravarmmā* (Dūbī seal, lines 8-9) and *śrī-Bhogavatyāṁ dvir = aśvamedhayājī śrī-Sthiravarmmā* (Nālandā seal, lines 6-7) while referring to the performance of the same sacrifices by Sthiravarman.

124. 'Aśvamedhas Performed by the Kings of Kāmarūpa', *IHQ*, XXI, 1945, pp. 144-45.

125. *Dviraśvamedhayājī śrī-Sthiravarmmā.*

126. *IAA*, p. 24, verse 24.

127. *Ibid.*, p. 41, verse 12.

128. Both these English renderings are quoted from *ibid.*, pp. 22 and 51.

129. This, and not 'the reviver of the Aśvamedha which had been in abeyance for long' as commonly held, is the correct interpretation of the phrase *chir-otsann-āśvamedh-āhartṛi* occurring in the Gupta inscriptions while referring to Samudra Gupta's Aśvamedhas. *Vide* V.S. Pathak, 'Notes on Gupta Coinage-I:II. Aśvamedha by Samudragupta', *JNSI*, XIX, 1957, pp. 142-44. The relevant passages from the *Śatapatha Brāhmaṇa* were cited earlier by J. Ph. Vogel while editing Mūlavarman's *yūpa* inscriptions from Borneo. Reference cited by B. Ch. Chhabra in his *Catalogue of the Gupta Gold Coins of the Bayana Hoard in the National Museum*, p. xxv and fn. 28.

130. Summarised from *Rāja-taraṅgiṇī*, II. 143-III. 2.

131. *Kalhaṇa's Rāja-taraṅgiṇī: A Chronicle of the Kings of Kaśmīr*, Engl. Translation, I, Chronological Table, p. 136.

132. *KŚ*, Part I, p. 37.

133. *Ibid.*, p. 25.

134. *Vide* chronological tables in Stein, *op. cit.*, pp. 134ff.

135. *Ibid.*, p. 136.

136. *Ibid.*, III. 103, p. 81.

137. For a general description of coins of Toramāṇa, see A. Cunningham, *Coins of Mediaeval India*, p. 42; V.A. Smith, *A Catalogue of Coins in the Indian Museum, Calcutta: Coins of Ancient India*, pp. 235-36.

138. *EHK*, pp. 45-46, 157.

139. *HCPA*, pp. 149-50.

140. *IAA*, p. 19.

141. *Rāja-taraṅgiṇī*, III. 8-10:

स मेघवननामानमग्रहारं विनिर्ममे।
मयुष्टकृत् पुण्यज्येष्ठं मेघमठं तदा।।
भोगाय देश्यभिक्षूणां वल्लभाऽस्यामृतप्रभा।
विहारमुच्चैरमृतभवनाख्यमकारयत्।।

देशैकदेशाल्लोनर्मिन: प्राप्तस्तस्या: पितुर्गुरु: ।
स्तुन्पा तद्भाषया प्रोक्तो लोस्तोन्पास्तूपकार्यकृत् ।।
This monastery known as Amṛitabhavana was known to the Chinese traveller Ou-K'ong. *Vide* Stein, *Rāja-taraṅgiṇī*, Engl. Tr., Introduction, p.82, and fn. (9) on verses 8-9 of Book III.

142. Some scholars have inferred from it that Buddhism was popular in Prāgjyotisha during the early centuries AD and that Balavarman (who is commonly identified with Meghavāhana's father-in-law) had embraced Buddhism under the inspiration of the Tibetan teacher in question. *Vide EHK*, pp. 44-46, 152; *HCPA*, 149-50, 430. This is, however, hotly refuted by M.M. Sharma who is baffled by the fact recorded in the two known charters of Bhāskaravarman that he was a devout worshipper of god Śiva and therefore could not have had a Buddhist scholar for his *guru* or spiritual teacher. Therefore he tries to interpret the relevant stanzas of the *Rāja-taraṅgiṇī* to obviate the apparent contradiction. *Vide IAA*, Introduction, pp. 18-21. We feel, however, that there is absolutely no contradiction in an ancient Indian ruler following one religion and patronising at the same time another religion and we have several such cases in ancient Indian history which are too well-known to brook reiteration.

143. Both Harshavardhana and Bhāskaravarman were staunch Śaivas and yet nothing deterred them from extending liberal patronage to Buddhism as recorded by Yuan Chwang and his biographer Shaman Hwui Li which has often been misconstrued by historians as an evidence of Harsha in his later life becoming a Buddhist.

144. J.F. Fleet, *CII*, III, pp. 146ff., verse 5.

145. *Vide* D.C. Sircar, *Select Inscriptions*, I, p. 419, fn. 3.

146. *Ibid.*, p. 203, verses 13-14.

147. For these allusions, see *IAA*, Introduction, pp. 15-18.

148. D.C. Sircar, 'Dūbī Plates of Bhāskaravarman', *EI*, XXX, 1953-54, pp. 287-304; *IAA*, pp. 10-32; *KŚ*, pp. 7-18, 152-60.

149. Padmanatha Bhattacharya, 'Nidhānpur Copper-Plates of Bhāskaravarman', *EI*, XII, 1913-14, pp. 65-79; 'Two Lost Plates of Nidhānpur Copper-Plates of Bhāskaravarman', *ibid.*, XIX, 1927-28, pp. 115-27; 'A Third Lost Plate of the Nidhānpur Plates of Bhāskaravarman,' *ibid.*, pp. 245-50; *IAA*, pp. 38-81; *KŚ*, pp. 33-35, 161-66.

150. श्रीभूतिवर्म्मा प्रददौ द्विजेभ्यो येभ्य: परं शासनमाक्षतं तत् ।
भूय: समुज्ज्वाल्य ददौ तदर्थे श्रीभास्कर: सम्प्रति तेभ्य एव ।।
IAA, p. 19, verse 76.

151. चन्द्रपुरिविषये.... एतद्विषयान्त:पातिमयूरशाल्मलाग्रहारक्षेत्रं राज्ञा श्रीभूतिवर्म्मणा कृतं यत् तत् ताम्रपट्टाभावात् करदमिति महाराजेन ज्येष्ठभद्रान् विज्ञाप्य पुनरस्याभिनवताम्रपट्टकरणाय शासनं दष्टवा..... भूमिच्छिद्रन्यायेन पूर्व्वभोक्तृब्राह्मणेभ्य: प्रतिपादितं.....
IAA, p. 43, lines 49-54.

152. शासन-दाहादर्वागभिनव-भिन्नरूपाणि तेभ्यो अक्षराणि यस्मात् तस्मान्नैतानि कूटानि ।
Ibid., p. 49, lines 139-40.

This statement, which amounts to too much of a defene, raises suspicion about the genuineness of this charter.

It appears that the destruction of original documents and their substitution by fresh documents was a common feature in the region and we have some such recorded instances in subsequent period as well. For some of these *vide* R. D. Choudhury, *Catalogue of the Inscriptions in the Assam State Museum*, Nos. ASM 5081, 5089, 4097, etc.

153. *Ibid.* , p. 19, lines 112-17, for the names of the donees. It must be stated here that some of the names are either only partially preserved or lost.

154. *Ibid.*, pp. 43-48, lines 54-126 (text). For a consolidated list together with details of the Vedic *śākhās, gotras, etc.*, *vide ibid.*, pp. 76-81. See appendix to this chapter for the list extracted from this work.

155. In the three generations of the original donees that must have intervened between the original donees and the beneficiaries named in the records in question, as between the original donor and the renewer of the charters, the donees must have multiplied manifold, at least three or four times.

156. *Vide IAA*, p. 41, lines 2-3:
Svasti mahā-nau-hasty-aśva-patti-saṁpatty-upātta-jaya-śabd-ānvartha-skandhāvārāt Karṇṇasuvarṇa-vāsakāt.

157. *Vide* D.C. Sircar, *Indian Epigraphical Glossary*, p. 314, s. v. *skandhāvāra.*

158. For strong arguments favouring the connotation 'capital' and inscriptional parallels, *vide IAA*, pp. 58-59.

159. Various identifications of the town of Karṇasuvarṇa have been proposed by scholars. Alexander Cunningham (*Ancient Geography of India*, pp. 425-26) thought of locating it 'along the course of the Suvarṇa-ṛiksha river, somewhere about the districts of Singhbhum and Barabhum' (Bīrbhūm). He further observed, 'Barā Bāzār is the chief town in Barabhum, and as its position corresponds very closely with that indicated by Hwen Thsang, it may be accepted as the approximate site of the capital in the seventh century'. James Fergusson (*History of India*, p. 248), however, does not find this location acceptable and instead suggested that the kingdom of Karṇasuvarṇa comprehended the northern part of Burdwan, the whole of Birbhum, and the province of Murshidabad, including all those parts of the districts of Krishnanagar and Jessore which were then sufficiently raised above the waters of the Ganges to be inhabitable. However, in view of the statement of the Chinese pilgrim that the monastery of the 'Red clay' (Raktamṛittikā) was located close to it, the town must have been situated in the proximity of Raṅgāmātī in the Murshidābād district of West Bengal.

159a. K.N. Gupta takes for granted the reading of the village of the granted land as Brahmottara and attempts its location. *Vide* his 'Identification of Brahmottara', *IHQ*, VII, 1931, pp. 743-46.

160. *IAA*, p. 43, lines 49-51.

160a. The name is spelt both as Gaṅgaṇikā and Gaṅgiṇikā in the inscription and no significance attaches to this minor difference as such small differences are fairly common in ancient epigraphs.

161. *Ibid.*, p. 49, lines 128-32.

162. For the Khalīmpur charter, see F. Kielhorn, 'Khalīmpur Plate of Dharmapāla', *EI*, IV, 1896-97, pp. 243-54. For the references to Gaṅgiṇikā and the village called Māḍhaśāmmalī, see *ibid.*, p. 249, lines 32 and 37 respectively.
163. *Ibid.*, XIX, 1927-28, p. 117. For details of Bhattacharya's view expressed in his *Kāmarūpa-śāsanāvali* in this matter, see *IAA*, pp. 59-60.
164. *EI*, XIX, p. 117, fn. 2. For the relevant text, see *IAA*, p. 100, verse 33 and line 21. But the reading given in the original publication in the *JASB*, IX, 1840, is Chandrapari, not Chandrapuri.
165. *EHK*, pp. 50-51. Also some papers included in his *SEHA*.
166. *HCPA*, pp. 158-64.
167. *IAA*, pp. 62-64.
168. *KS*, Part I, pp. 40-41.
169. R.G. Basak, 'The Five Dāmodarpur Copper-Plate Inscriptions of the Gupta Period', *EI*, XV, 1919-20, pp. 113-45.
170. *Vide ibid.*, No. 1, p. 130, lines 2-3; No. 2, p. 133, line 2; No. 3, pp.135-36, lines 1-2; No. 4, p. 138, line 2; No. 5, p.142, lines 1-2. Also *ibid.*, p. 130, line 1.
171. *Ibid.*, p. 133, line 1.
172. *Ibid.*, pp. 135-36; 138-39.
173. Of the date of No. 3 (of Budha Gupta) only the unit figure of 3 is preserved fully, while the middle figure has been doubtfully restored as 20, so that we can aver that the date included the figure 23, while the hundred figure is altogether lost, which makes the determination of its exact date difficult. Of No. 5 (also of Budha Gupta) the figure for year is completely damaged.
174. Only the surname (Gupta) is preserved. It has been suggested doubtfully by Basak that this (first) component may have been Bhānu, probably because the equation is chronologically very likely in view of the fact that he is known to have died in AD 510. *Vide ibid.*, p. 142, fn. 1.
175. *Vide HCIP*, III: *CA*, Chronology, p. 698.
176. *EI*, XV, p. 142, line 1.
177. By oversight Basak has equated it with AD 433-34 instead of with 533-34. *Vide ibid.*, p. 142.
178. Bhattacharya cites as an example of a charter being found far away from the donated land the Kamauli plates of Vaidyadeva which record donation of land in Assam but were found near Varanasi. See *EI*, XII, 1913-14, p. 66. For the Kamauli plates, see Arthur Venis, 'Copper-Plate Grant of Vaidyadeva, King of Kāmarūpa', *ibid.*, II, 1894, pp. 347-58. To it one may add two other well-known examples, viz. (i) the Puṇe plates of the Vākāṭaka queen Prabhāvatī Guptā which, though belonging to the Hiṅgaṇghāṭ region of Vidarbha originally, were found with a resident of Pune, and (ii) the Indore plates of the Vākāṭaka king Pravara Sena II recording the grant of land in the Balaghat region of Vidarbha. All these had travelled to these far off localities with the descendants of the beneficiaries of the charters or with those who had their possession for some or other reason. But ordinarily we must look for the locale of the donated land in the area close to the provenance.
179. 'Grant of Bhāskara Varman of Kāmarūpa and the Nāgara Brāhmaṇas', *IHQ*, VI, 1930, pp. 60-71.

180. *Coper-Plates of Sylhet*, p.56ff.
181. *Early History of Bengal*, p. 26.
182. Amarnath Ray, 'Nagar Brahmans and Sylhet', *IC*, I, 1933, pp. 698-700.
183. Jogendra Chandra Ghosh, 'Donated Land of the Nidhanpur Charter of Bhāskaravarman of Kāmarūpa', *ibid.*, II, 1935, pp. 153-57; *Some Castes and Caste Origin in Sylhet*, Assam Census Report, 1931, Appendix C, pp. xxii-xxvii. Cited by P.C. Choudhury in his *HCPA*, p. 159 and fn. 96.
184. *IA*, LXI, pp. 41-55; D.R. Bhandarkar's review of K.L. Barua's *Early History of Kāmarūpa*, *IC*, I, 1933, pp. 136-37.
185. 'Location of the Land granted by the Nidhānpur Grant of Bhākaravarmmā of Kāmarūpa', *JASB*, 1935, pp. 419ff.; 'New Light on the History of Assam', *IHQ*, XXI, 1945, pp. 26-27. See also K.N. Gupta, 'Identification of Brahmottara', *ibid.*, VII, 1931, pp. 743-46 for the same view.
186. The whole problem has been discussed threadbare together with full references to different views on the subject by P.C. Choudhury (*HCPA*, pp. 157-64) and M.M. Sharma (*IAA*, pp. 59-64) though we do not agree with their view.
187. M. Pauthier (translator), 'Thien-chu - India: Extract from Ma-twa-lin, Book CCCXXXVIII. Fol. 14', translated from the French of M. Stanislas Julien, *IA*, 1880, p. 17.

     Although the English translator is not named with the caption, there is circumstantial evidence to indicate that the translation was done by M. Pauthier. See *ibid.*, p. 14, fn. 1.
188. The Chinese word meaning 'loved by the moon' has been rendered in Sanskrit by 'Chandrapriya'. But as there are several words in Sanskrit for both 'moon' and 'loved', the name under reference could also have been a different one.
189. It has now turned into Kundu.
190. At present we have the surname Gān.
191. Dhara has now become Dar.
192. In the form Deb.
193. 'Nagar Brāhmaṇas and the Bengal Kāyasthas', *IA*, LXI, pp. 61-75. B.K. Barua (*CHA*, p. 106) observes that the donees of the Nidhānpur charter were brāhmaṇas from Nagarkot.
194. R.G. Basak, 'Tipperah Copper-plate Grant of Lokanātha, the 44th Year', *EI*, XV, 1919-20, pp. 301-15. For the list of the donees together with details of their *gotras* and the Vedas, see *ibid.*, pp. 312-15.
195. The charter (*IAA*, p. 100, line 19) was issued from a locality whose name has been read variously as Hāṭakeśvara or Hārūppeśvara which was evidently named after the god of that name.
196. *IAA*, p. 48, line 126.
197. *HCPA*, pp. 336-37.
198. *IAA*, p. 43, lines 50-51.
199. *Indian Epigraphical Glossary*, p. 10.
200. *Ibid.*, p. 11.
201. This is shown by his inclusion of only such terms for entries in his *Glossary*.
202. It is also met with in the Nirmaṇḍ plate of the Mahāsāmanta Samudrasena.

Vide J.F. Fleet, *Inscriptions of the Gupta Kings and their Successors, CII*, III, p. 289, line 10 (*dev-āgrāhāra*).

203. See K.V. Ramesh and S.P. Tiwari, *A Copper-Plate Hoard of the Gupta Period from Bagh, Madhya Pradesh*, p. 42, line 5; p. 56, line 5; p. 60, line 2. Also see numerous allied expressions cited below.
204. All the Parivrājaka inscriptions referring to the creation of brāhmaṇa settlements spell the word as *agrāhāra*. *Vide* J.F. Fleet, *CII*, III, p. 103, line 16: *Korpparik-āgrāhāra*; p. 108, line 10: *agāhāra*; p. 122, line 8: *dev- āgrāhāra*.
205. K.V. Ramesh and S.P. Tiwari, *op. cit.*, p. 40, line 5.
206. *Ibid.*, p. 31, line 6; p. 48, line 5.
207. *Ibid.*, p. 17, line 4.
208. *Ibid.*, p. 42, line 6.
209. *Ibid.*, p. 11, line 4; p. 22, line 5.
210. *Ibid.*, p. 11, line 6; p. 13, line 7; p. 20, line 8; p. 22, line 7; p. 26, lines 6-7.
211. *Ibid.*, p. 11, line 4.
212. *Ibid.*, p. 8, line 4; p. 9, line 8; p. 20, line 4; p. 26, line 5.
213. *Ibid.*, p. 13, lines 4-5.
214. *Ibid.*, p. 55, line 2.
215. *Ibid.*, p. 37, line 3.

APPENDIX I

TEXT OF THE DŪBĪ SEAL

1. श्री**मान्नरकतनयो भगदत्तवज्रदत्तान्वयो** महाराजा-
2. धिराजश्रीप्राग्ज्योतिषेन्द्र**पुष्यवर्म्मा** तत्पुत्रो महाराजाधिरा-
3. जश्री**समुद्रवर्म्मा** तस्य तनयो दत्तदेव्यां महाराजाधिराज-
4. श्रीव(**ब**)**लवर्म्मा** तेन[1] जातो देव्यां श्रीरत्नवत्यां महाराजाधिराज-
5. श्री**कल्याणवर्म्मा** श्रीगधर्व्ववत्यां श्री**गणपतिवर्म्मा** श्रीय-
6. ज्ञवत्यां श्री**महेन्द्रो** द्विस्तुरगमेधाहर्त्ता श्रीसुव्रतायां श्री**नारा-**
7. **यणवर्म्मा** श्रीदेवमत्यां श्री**भूतिवर्म्मा** श्रीविज्ञानवत्यां श्री-
8. **चन्द्रमुखवर्म्मा** श्रीभोगवत्यां द्विरश्वमेधया-
9. जी श्री**स्थिरवर्म्मा** तेन[2] श्रीनारायणायां श्री-
10. **सुस्थितवर्म्मा** तेन श्रीध्रुवलक्ष्म्यां
11. श्री**भास्करवर्म्मेति [।।*]**[3]

NOTES AND REFERENCES

1. *Tasmāj jātaḥ* should be the correct expression.
2. As above, the expression here also ought to be *tasmāt*.
3. Based on D.C. Sircar's reading in *EI*, XXX, 1953-54, p. 288. The illustration, facing p. 305 is almost totally illegible.

APPENDIX II

THE NĀLANDĀ SEAL OF BHĀSKARAVARMAN

1. श्रीमन्**नरकतनयो**[1] **भगदत्तवज्रदत्तान्वयो** महाराजाधिराजश्रीप्राग्ज्योतिषे-
2. न्द्रः **पुष्यवर्म्मा** तत्पुत्रो महाराजाधिराजः श्री**समुद्रवर्म्मा** तस्य तनयो दत्तवत्यां[2]
3. महाराजाधिराजश्री**बलवर्म्मा** तेन जातो देव्यां श्रीरत्नवत्यां महाराजाधिरा-
4. जश्री**कल्याणवर्म्मा** श्रीगन्धर्ववत्यां श्री**गणपतिवर्म्मा** श्रीयज्ञवत्यां श्री**महे-**
5. **न्द्रवर्म्मा** दिस्तुरगमेधाहर्त्ता श्रीसुव्रतायां श्री**नारायणवर्म्मा** श्रीदे-
6. वमत्यां श्री**भूतिवर्म्मा**[3] श्रीविज्ञानवत्यां श्री**चन्द्रमुखवर्म्मा** श्रीभो-
7. गवत्यां द्विरश्वमेधयाजी श्री**स्थिरवर्म्मा** तेन श्रीनयनशोभायां
8. श्री**सुस्थिरवर्म्मा** तेन श्रीध्रुवलक्ष्म्यां[4] श्री**सुप्रतिष्ठितवर्म्म**-
9. श्री**भास्करवर्म्मेति**[5]

NOTES AND REFERENCES

1. M.M. Sharma reads *śrīmān* instead of *śrīman* (with short *a)* which is seen clearly in the plate given by Sastri.
2. Some fragments of Nālandā seals reported in 1917-18 prefix the word-form *mahā* (from *mahat*) to this name, viz. the name with the honorific *śrīmat* is spelt as *śrīmad-* Mahābhūtivarmmā.
3. For these seals K.N. Dikshit suggests to read *śrī-Śyāmalakshmyāṁ*.
4. This is the consolidated reading of all seal-fragments.
5. This is based, generally speaking, on Hirananda Sastri, *Nalanda and its Epigraphical Material* and M.M. Sharma, *IAA*, p. 34.

APPENDIX III

DONEES OF THE NIDHĀNPUR PLATES OF BHĀSKARAVARMAN

Sr. No.	*Name*	*Veda*	*Gotra*	*Share*
1.	Sādhāraṇasvamin[1]	Vājasaneya (Yajurveda)	Prāchetasa	2
2-5.	Śrīvasu and his 3 brothers	do.	do.	1
6-7.	Somavasu and his brother	do.	do.	½
8.	Manoratha*s*	Chhandoga (Sāmaveda)	Kātyāya	1 ¾
9.	Vishṇughosha*s*	do.	do.	½
10.	Vedaghosha*s*	do.	do.	1
11.	Dāmodara*s*	Bahvṛich (Ṛigveda)	Yāska	1
12.	Ghoshadeva*s*	do.	do.	½
13.	Nandadeva*s*	do.	do.	½
14.	Arkadatta & clan	Chhandoga	Bhāradvāja	1½
15.	Tushṭidatta*s*	do.	do.	½
16.	Ṛishidāmaa*s*	Vājasaneyī	Kāśyapa	1
17.	Śubhadāma*s*	do.	do.	1
18.	Śanaiścharabhūti & clan	do.	Kautsa	1
19.	Saṅkarshaṇa*s*	Bahvṛich	Gaurātreya	2
20.	Nara*s*	do.	do.	1
21.	Nārāyaṇa*s*	do.	do.	½
22.	Vishṇu*s*	do.	do.	1
23.	Sudarśana*s*	do.	do.	1
24.	Gopendra*s*	do.	do.	1
25.	Arka*s*	do.	do.	¼
26.	Bhānu*s*	do.	do.	½
27.	Bhūyaskara*s*	do.	do.	½
28.	Yaśobhūti*s* & clan	Vājasaneya	Kṛishṇātreya	1
29.	Varuṇa*s*	Chhandoga	Bhāradvāja	1
30.	Madhusena*s*	Vājasaneya	Kauṇḍinya	1
31.	Dhruvasoma*s*	Chhandoga	Gautama	1
32.	Vishṇusoma*s*	do.	do.	1
33.	Vishṇupālita*s*	Vājasaneya	Bhāradvāja	1½
34.	Śuchipālita*s*	do.	do.	1
35-36.	Mitrapālita & Arthapālita	do.	do.	½
37.	Prajāpālita*s*	do.	Bhāradvāja	¼

Sr. No.	Name	Veda	Gotra	Share
38.	Madhus	Vājasaneya	Ġautama	1
39.	Chakradevas	do.	do.	½
40.	Kushmāṇḍapatras	Charaka (Yajurveda)	Vatsa	3/16
41.	Īśvaradattas	do.	Maudgalya	2
42-43.	Sudarśana & Dinakaras	Vājasaneya	do.	1
44.	Yajñakuṇḍas	do.	Śaubha (or na)ka	1½
45.	Yaśaḥkuṇḍas	do.	do.	1¼
46.	Śrāddhakuṇḍas	do.	do.	1
47.	Nārāyaṇakuṇḍas	do.	do.	1
48.	Īśvarakuṇḍas	do.	do.	1⅛
49.	Śaktikuṇḍas	do.	do.	¼
50.	Toshakuṇḍas	do.	do.	1⅛
51.	Sādhus	Charaka	Pārāśarya	1
52.	Gaṅgāas	Chhandoga	Āsvalāyana	1
53.	Naras	Bahvṛich	Vārāha	1
54.	Pravaranāgas	do.	do.	¾
55.	Apanāgas	do.	do.	1
56-57.	Toshanāga & Haṁsanāgas	do.	do.	¼
58.	Mānaghoshas	Vājasda-saneyīa	Kāśyapa	1
59.	Sarpiṇīs	Chhandoga vṛiddhi	Vaishṇa-	1
60.	Janārdanas	do.	do.	1
61.	Arkas	Bahvṛich	Kauśikā	1½
62.	Śradhadāsas	do.	do.	½
63.	Sanātanas	Vājasaneja	Gautama	1
64.	Harshaprabha & clan	do.	do.	½
65.	Khaṇḍasomas	do.	Kauṭilya	1½
66-68	Śreyaskara, Gati & Gaurisoma	Vājasaneya	do.	1
69.	Vakulasomas	do.	do.	½
70-71.	Dhṛitasoma & Siṁhasomas	do.	do.	½
72.	Bhāyaśaḥs	do.	Kṛishṇātreya	½
73.	Yajñas	do.	do.	1¼
74.	Daivas	do.	do.	1¼
75.	Dardis	do.	do.	½
76.	Pradyumnas	do.	do.	1½

Sr. No.	Name	Veda	Gotra	Share
77.	Vṛiddhas	Vājasaneya	Kṛishṇātreya	2
78-82.	Divākara, Hari, Adbhuta and Toshanāga	do.	do.	1
83.	Medhas	do.	Kavestara	1
84.	Dhṛitis & clan	do.	Māṇḍavya	¼
85.	Keśavas	do.	Kāśyapa	1
86.	Gauris	Vājasaneya	Bhāradvāja	1
87.	Sucharitas	do.	do.	½
88.	Vappas	do.	do.	1
89.	Karkadattas	Bahvṛich	Kauṇḍinya	1
90.	Udayanas	do.	Bhāradvāja	1
91.	Merudattas	do.	Vasishṭha	1
92-93.	Narendra & Reṇubhūtis	Vājasaneya	Agniveśya	1
94.	Medhabhūtis	do.	do.	½
95.	Chandrapakshas	Charaka	Sāṅkṛit-yāyana	1
96.	Kalis	Bahvṛich	Yāska	1
97.	Svāmin (?)	do.	do.	1½
98.	Bhaṭṭimaheśvaras	do.	do.	½
99.	Gopālanandis	do.	Parāśara	1
100.	Viśvabhūtis	do.	Bhārgava	1
101-2.	Surañjitas & Sucharitras	do.	do.	½
103.	Śivagaṇas	Taittirīya (Yajurveda)	Bhāradvāja	1
104-7.	Vasuśrīs & brothers	Bahvṛich	Kātyāyana	1
108.	Vīrabhūtis	Vājasaneya	Kauśikā	1
109.	Vishṇubhūtis	do.	do.	½
110.	Pramodabhūtis	do.	do.	1
111.	Vishṇudattas	do	Bhāradvāja	1
112.	Bṛihaspatis	do.	Kauṇḍinya	1
113.	Harshadevas	Bahvṛich	Yāska	1
114.	Medhas	Vājasaneya	Jātūkarṇa	1
115.	Kṛishṇas	do.	do.	1
116-17.	Mādhava & Hari	do.	do.	1
118.	Janārdanadevas	Chhandoga	Bhāradvāja	1
119.	Vishṇusomas	Vājasaneya	Mudgala	½
120.	Dhanasenas	Charaka	Garga	1
121-22.	Pramodasena & Ghoshasena	do.	do.	1

Sr. No.	Name	Veda	Gotra	Share
123.	Somasenas	Charaka	Garga	1
124.	Bhāskaramitras	Bahvṛich	Gautama	1
125.	Madhumitras	do.	do.	1
126-27.	Sādhāraṇamitra & Sādhumitra	do.	do.	1
128.	Dhṛitimitras	do.	do.	½
129.	Śukrabhavas	do.	Bhāradvāja	1
130-31.	Sudarśana & Dhaneśvaras	do.	Pautrimāshya	½
132.	Ravis	Vājasaneya	Śāṇḍilya	1
133.	Madhus	do.	do.	1
134.	Mahīdharas	do.	do.	1
135.	Bhaṭṭimahāsenas	Bahvṛich	Pūrṇṇa	1
136.	Bhaṭṭimātṛis	do.	do.	½
137.	Rudrabhaṭṭis	do.	do.	½
138.	Adrivilepanas	Chhandoga	Kauśikā	1
139.	Gomināgas	Vājasaneya	Sāvarnika	1
140.	Sūryas	do.	Śālaṅkāyana	1
141.	Bhavadevas	do.	Bhāradvāja	1
142.	Śarvadevas	do.	do.	1
143.	Gomidevas	do.	do.	½
144.	Sāvitradevas	do.	do.	2
145.	Arkadevas	do.	do.	½
146.	Sādhāraṇas	do.	do.	¼
147.	Dāmarātas	do.	Garga	1
148.	Vasudattas	do.	Bhāradvāja	2
149.	Yāgeśvaras	do.	Ālambāyana	2
150.	Viśveśvaras	do.	do.	1
151.	Divyeśvaras	do.	do.	1
152.	Gaṇeśvaras	do.	do.	1
153.	Budheśvaras	do.	do.	1
154-55.	Jāteśvara & Aṅgeśvara	do.	do.	1
156.	Dhauteśvaras	do.	do.	¼
157.	Magheśvaras	do.	do.	¼
158.	Jahneśvaras	do.	do.	½
159.	Nandeśvaras	do.	do.	1
160.	Dāmabhūti	do.	Aṅgiras	1
161-62.	Prakāśavaras & his brother	Bahvṛich	Kāśyapa	1

Sr. No.	Name	Veda	Gotra	Share
163.	Gāyatrīpālas	Vājasaneya	Yāska	1
164.	Śāntaśarmas	Bahvṛich	Parāśara	1
165.	Padmadāsas & his clan	do.	Kauśikā	1
166-69.	Govardhana, Yajñapāla, Panu & Sudaraānas[2]	do.	do.	½
170.	Gopālas	Chhandoga	Paṅkala	1
171.	Ugradatta	Taittirīya	Kaśyapa	1
172.	Bhaṭṭinandas	Bahvṛich	Bārhaspatya	1
173.	Sādhus	do.	do.	1
174.	Devakulas	do.	do.	1
175.	Janārdanas	Bahvṛich	Bārhaspatya	½
176-78.	Sunayana, Nārāyaṇa & Vṛiddhis	do.	do.	½
179.	Iśvarabhaṭṭas	do.	Gautama	1
180.	Bhṛigus	do.	do.	½
181.	Rudraghoshas	do.	Bhāradvāja	1
182.	Kauśisomas	Charaka	Kātyāyana	1
183.	Prabhākarakīrtis	Vājasaneya	Gautama	1
184.	Anantas	do.	Śāṇḍilya	1
185.	Gatibhaṭṭis	Bahvṛich	Śaunaka	1
186.	Tejabhaṭṭis	do.	do.	1
187-89.	Managhosha, Tejabhaṭṭi & Nandabhūtis[3]	do.	do.	½
190.	Dāmabhaṭṭis	do.	do.	1
191.	Medhabhaṭṭis	do.	do.	1
192.	Sumatibhaṭṭis	do.	do.	1
193.	Suyogabhaṭṭis	do.	do.	1
194.	Śāśvatadāmas	do.	Vātsya	1
195.	Toshas	Chhandoga	Gautama	1
196.	Bhaṭṭiharas	Bahvṛich	Varāha	1
197.	Nāgadattas	Vājasaneya	Bhāradvāja	½
198-99.	Dāruveshas & his brother	do.	Ālambāyana	½
200.	Rūpāḍhyas	do.	Bhāradvāja	½
201-2.	Chandradāsas & Vimardanadāsas	Bahvṛich	Kauśikā	1
203.	Supratishṭhitas	Vājasaneya	Kaśyapa	1
204.	Nandanas	do.	Gautama	1

Sr. No.	*Name*	*Veda*	*Gotra*	*Share*
205.	Toshas	Vājasaneya	Śākaṭāyana	½
206-7.	Sārasa & Vakulas	Vājasaneya	Gautama & Kaśyapa	1
208.	Vidūshas	do.	Bhāradvāja	½

Note: In addition to these, 7 portions were given for *bali, charu* and *sattra.*[4]

NOTES AND REFERENCES

1. The word *svāmin* occurs at the end of almost all the names like an honorific and has therefore been abbreviated as *s*.
2. There seem to be intended these four donees and the use of the dual number is an inadvertent error instead of the plural number.
3. In lines 118-19 dual number is employed instead of the desired plural number.
4. This table has been adapted from M.M. Sharma's *IAA*, pp. 76-81, with only necessary modifications.

Chapter III

KUMĀRA BHĀSKARAVARMAN AND AFTER

1. KUMĀRA ALIAS BHĀSKARAVARMAN

Bhāskaravarman, the last known member of the Bhauma-Nāraka or Varman dynasty, was also the most brilliant star of the politico-cultural horizon of ancient Prāgjyotisha. In association with his esteemed friend Harshavardhana of Sthāṇvīśvara (Thanesar, Kurukshetra district, Haryana) and Kānyakubja (Kannauj, Farrukhabad district, Uttar Pradesh) he played a very vital role in contemporary Indian political and religious sphere. In fact, in documented historical times he was the first, and perhaps the only, Prāgjyotisha monarch to play such a dominant role on a pan-India level. And we are fortunate in having non-Prāgjyotisha sources of information about his activities thanks to Harshavardhana's poet laureate Bāṇabhaṭṭa and the Chinese sources including the *Si-yu-ki* of Yuan Chwang, the *Life* by Shaman Hwui Li, the *She-kia-fang-che* as well as the *Ma-twa-lin* which supply a rich mass of data for his reign as against most of the earlier members of the dynasty who are known exclusively from epigraphs localised in Prāgjyotisha without any other corroboration from any other source.

Kumāra: Another Name

He was also known to his contemporaries as Kumāra. Bāṇabhaṭṭa, the court-poet of Harshavardhana and the author of his biographical romance entitled *Harsha-charita*, refers to him more often by this name. Thus, the chamberlain (*pratīhāra*) announcing to Harsha the arrival of Haṁsavega, the envoy (*dūta*) of the Prāgjyotisha king refers to him as Kumāra.[1] While inquiring about the well-being of Bhāskaravarman from Haṁsavega, Harsha speaks of him by this name.[2] He is represented as mentioning Bhāskaravarman by the same name while appreciating the miraculous umbrella of Varuṇa sent to him as present.[3] And he expresses to Haṁsavega his anxiousness of seeing his master Kumāra.[4] And, finally we are told that Bhāskaravarman was Kumāra's other name.[5] In the Chinese sources also Bhāskaravarman is often mentioned as Kumāra or Kumāra-rāja though they are also aware of the former name. Thus, his contemporary Chinese pilgrim and friend Yuan Chwang informs us that Bhāskaravarman was styled Kumāra.[6] Elsewhere while describing Kāmarūpa we are told that 'his other name' was 'Kumāra'.[7] Shaman Hwui Li, the biographer of Yuan Chwang, refers to him frequently by the name Kumāra-rāja.[8] The same name (Kumāra-rāja) is used for him in the *She-kia-fang-che*.[9] Book CCCXXXVIII, Fol. 14 of the *Ma-twa-lin* speaks of him as Shi-kieu-ma which has been transliterated doubtfully as Śrīkumāra.[10] It appears that he had both the names, viz. Kumāra and Bhāskaravarman, which people employed according to their preference.[11] In view of this fact it is indeed strange that some historians including P.N. Bhattacharya,[12] K.L. Barua[13] and P.C. Choudhury[14] have preferred to treat Kumāra as a title of Bhāskaravarman. A better explanation of this name has recently been suggested by Jai Prakash Singh who is of the opinion that he was a crown prince (*kumāra*) under his elder brother and royal predecessor Supratishṭhitavarman and that the title may have continued to be employed for him even after he himself became a king.[14a]

Date of Accession

We are fortunate in that we have dependable evidence about the period of his rule, the exact limits of his reign can not be ascertained though. The extant evidence in the form of Bāṇa's description of the visit of Kumāra's emissary Haṁsavega to Harshavardhana which shows that shortly after his accession to the throne in AD 606 when he was on his way to punish the Gauḍa king Śaśāṅka came Haṁsavega to convey his master's errand of undying friendship and there is no doubt left that Bhāskaravarman was already on the throne at that time. And that he is reported to have played a vital role in the Chinese raid following his ally Harsha's death (AD 647-48) would show that his long reign covered practically the whole of the first half of the seventh century AD. It is not impossible that, as suggested by some historians, he came to power a few years prior to A.D 600.[15]

Extraction

Yuan Chwang would have us believe that Kumāra Bhāskaravarman was 'a brāhmin by caste'.[16] However, the name-ending *varman* of all the monarchs right from the time of the first king Pushyavarman is enough to show that they themselves believed in (or claimed to) their being kshatriyas. It is not unlikely that he and his ancestors actually belonged to the Indo-Mongoloid Boḍo stock as conjectured by S.K. Chatterjee.[17] But in all likelihood, they hailed from an autochthonous Assamese stock and were conferred the kshatriya (or brāhmaṇa) status and descent from the line of Bhagadatta of the epic fame by their brāhmaṇa priests.

Alliance with Harsha and the Gauḍa Śaśāṅka

Bhāskaravarman ascended the throne of Kāmarūpa at a very critical moment in her history. As we have seen above, the Aphsaḍ (Shahabad district, Bihar) inscription of Ādityaseme, Aptnad inscription of the Later Gupta king Ādityasena informs us that his ancestor Mahāsena-gupta had worsted king Susthitavarman, father of Bhāskaravarman, and that the songs of his fame on account of this victory were sung by the Siddha couples on the banks of the river Lauhitya (Brahmaputra).[18] Susthitavarman probably did not survive this catastrophe long and left the kingdom in disarray, his two sons Supratishṭhitavarman, also known as Aridamanendra,[19] and Bhāskaravarman being too young to bear the onerous burden of administration. And just then came the Gauḍa invasion. The Dūbī plates of Bhāskaravarman inform us that shortly after Susthitavarman's demise the Gauḍas launched a powerful naval attack against Kāmarūpa and even though the two brothers fought valiantly they were carried away in an unconscious state to the Gauḍa capital as captives but later released and reinstated in their kingdom by the enemies,[20] evidently on their accepting the Gauḍa allegiance though it is not averred explicitly in the inscription. As the war took place during the short reign of Supratishṭhitavarman who was succeeded by his younger brother Bhāskaravarman sometime prior to AD 606, this event must have occurred in the closing years of the sixth or at the commencement of the seventh century AD, the precise date being unascertainable. Widely divergent views have been expressed as regards the identity of the Gauḍa invader. Some have proposed to identify him with the Later Gupta king Mahāsenagupta, who had defeated Susthitavarman shortly before[21] and others with Śaśāṅka or his immediate predecessor.[22] The former theory is, however, rendered untenable by the fact that neither Mahāsenagupta nor, for that matter, any other Later Gupta chief is ever styled a Gauḍa despite the fact that we have a fairly good number of his family records.[23] As against this Śaśāṅka is repeatedly referred to as a Gauḍa king in the *Harsha-charita*.[24]

As stated above, Bhāskaravarman succeeded his elder brother sometime in or before AD 606. Almost the first thing that the new king did after his accession was to throw off the Gauḍa allegiance, and as one of the means of safeguarding his newly won independence, sought an undying friendship with the emperor Harsha as indicated by the reported statement of his envoy, Haṁsavega, that his master was firmly determined never to pay homage to any being except Lord Śiva.[25] The alliance was evidently aimed at curbing the growing power of their common enemy Śaśāṅka, an objective that was achieved remarkably well, as we shall see presently.

The Gauḍa expedition undertaken by Harsha immediately after his accession probably resulted in the discomfiture of Śaśāṅka who was, however, permitted to rule his kingdom as a vassal as may be justifiably inferred from the late Buddhist text *Ārya-Mañjuśrī-mūla-kalpa* which avers that accompanied by a large army, king H[25a] (Harsha) attacked Puṇḍra and defeated king Soma[25b] (Śaśāṅka), the pursuer of wicked deeds, and forbade him to move out of his own country, ordering him to remain confined therein, and returned having been honoured in that kingdom.[26] There is no reason to suspect the veracity of this statement. In that case it is not improbable that the Rohtāsgaḍh seal-matrix[27] referring to Śaśāṅka as a *mahāsāmanta* (great feudatory) actually belongs to the period of his vassalage under Harsha.[28] However, Śaśāṅka could not reconcile that easily to a subordinate status for long and soon thereafter declared his independence as clearly vouched for by the Ganjām copperplate charter of his Śailodbhava feudatory Mādhavarāja II Sainyabhīta, dated Gupta year 600 (AD 619), wherein his overlord (Śaśāṅka) is styled *mahārājādhirāja*.[29] Harsha had consequently no option but to undertake a second expedition, this time together with his ally Bhāskaravarman, which proved fatal to their common adversary Śaśāṅka as we are informed by the *She-kia-fang-che*, an anonymous Chinese text composed around AD 650. 'The king (Śīlāditya),' we are told, 'with Kumāra-rāja ***destroyed*** the heretical king Śaśāṅka, his army and followers'.[30] Unfortunately, the exact date of this campaign can not be determined for want of requisite evidence, but it must have taken place sometime between AD 619, when Śaśāṅka was at the height of his power, and AD 631, when his erstwhile Śailodbhava feudatory had disowned his suzerainty and started ruling independently, evidently following the discomfiture of his former overlord at the hands of the combined forces of Śīlāditya (Harsha) and Kumāra-rāja (Bhāskaravarman).[31] The date of this event may be pushed a little earlier if we were to concede the assertion of the *Mañjuśrī-mūlakalpa* that Śaśāṅka's rule lasted just a little over seventeen years.[32]

The vast empire of the Gauḍa king Śaśāṅka comprising Bengal, Orissa and Magadha, now lay prostrate before the victors, viz. Harsha Śīlāditya and Bhāskaravarman Kumāra-rāja. There is no help coming from our sources as to how the victors disposed of this vast stretch of newly acquired territory with the result that vastly conflicting opinions are held by historians and it is just impossible to arrive at any final conclusion in this matter. But in the present state of our knowledge it looks most likely that Harsha occupied the whole of Śaśāṅka's kingdom, excepting only Koṅgoda or South Orissa which became independent and had to be conquered separately. The Nidhanpur plates of Bhāskaravarman issued from his capital or victorious camp at Karṇasuvarṇa, the former capital of Śaśāṅka,[33] indicate probably the transfer of the same territory to him following Harsha's demise.[34] However, the possibility of a partition of the conquered kingdom between the two allies also can not be ruled out altogether. In that case, Bhāskaravarman may have got as his share of the spoils the area lying to the east of the Gaṅgā,[35] the remainder of the territory being annexed by Harsha.[36]

Extent of Kingdom

The extant evidence indicates that Bhāskaravarman's kingdom included practically the whole of what was commonly known as Prāgjyotisha including the modern states of Assam and those carved out of it in recent years. In the *Harsha-charita* he is referred to as the king of Prāgjyotisha (*Prāgjyotish-eśvara*), and the same title is employed for him and many other members of the dynasty in its own records.[37] The Nidhānpur plates prove indisputably the inclusion of the Surma valley (Sylhet region) as an ancestral possession and of a large portion of Bengal, probably towards the close of his life, while the incorporation of the Kāmrūp region is indicated by his Dūbī plates. The Nowgong region is known to have formed part of the dominions of his family from much earlier times as Bindicated by the provenance of Bhūtivarman's Baḍgaṅgā rock inscription.[38] It appears from the *Si-yu-ki* of Yuan Chwang,[39] *The Life*,[40] and some other Chinese sources that on the east Bhaākaravarman's dominions touched the borders of

Burma and China. And if we are to believe what Shaman Hwui Li has put in the mouth of Bhāskaravasrman it would follow that he, and perhaps some of his predecessors, controlled the southern sea-route to China as well. When in response to Bhāskaravarman's repeated requests to stay on in India Yuan Chwang expressed his determination to leave for his motherland, the Kāmarūpa king offered to send official attendants to escort him if he preferred to go by the Southern Sea route.[41] He was indeed the greatest ruler of eastern India of his times, and the title of 'the King of Eastern India' applied to him in the Chinese works[42] is fully justified. And if one were asked to choose two greatest Indian rulers of the first half of the seventh cenury AD, the choice would naturally fall on Harshardhana and Kumāra Bhāskaravarman, both politically and culturally.

Bhāskara's Religious Policy, Buddhism and Yuan Chwang

The Dūbī and Nidhānpur plates of Bhāskaravarman himself and his errand conveyed to Harsha by his messenger Haṁsavega as reported by Bāṇa leave no doubt that he was a devout Śaiva. But in conformity with ancient Indian tradition of sectarian catholicity he extended patronage to the votaries of other religions as well. Buddhism claimed his special attention. Yuan Chwang avers that though 'not a Buddhist he treated accomplished śramaṇas with respect'.[43] It was out of his great love for Buddhism and enlightened curiosity about new ideas that he invited the Chinese pilgrim to visit him. As he was preparing to return to China and wanted to spend some time again at Nālandā (where he was then staying) before that he was not willing to concede the request but ultimately yielded on the advice of the old Buddhist teacher Śīlabhadra who was then the head of the Nālandā monastery. This is what Yuan Chwang himself avers.[44] But his biographer Hwui Li makes the event highly dramatic by adding that after two of his entreaties to Śīlabhadra proved futile he threw a challenge to him either to send Yuan Chwang on to him or face the destruction of the great monastery. As expected, this yielded the desired result and Śīlabhadra persuaded the Chinese pilgrim to pay a visit to the Kāmarūpa king. And he accompanied the envoy to Kāmarūpa.[45]

Bhāskara, a Subordinate Ally of Harsha

And just when he was sojourning in Kāmarūpa spending his days with the king, king Śīlāditya (Harsha), who was then returning to his capital after a successful expedition of Kung-yu-ta (Koṅgoda) and was then in the district of 'Kadjoughira' (equated with Kajangala, modern Rajmahals), heard of the Chinese priest having gone to king Kumāra. He sent summons to the latter 'to repair to him with his foreign guest, and when he replied with a refusal, saying that the king could take his head but not his guest', prompt came the retort, 'I trouble you for your head'. 'Thereupon', we are told, 'Kumāra became ***submissive***, and proceeded with the pilgrim and a grand retinue to join Śīlāditya.'[46] This event has also been dramatised by Hwui Li who narrates how Śīlāditya felt offended by the language of the reply of Kumāra and promptly sent the response, 'Send the head, that I may have it immediately by my messenger who is to bring it here.' He also gives the details of the retinue which included, besides his ministers, an army of 20,000 elephants and 30,000 ships.[47] A detailed account of their meeting is also given. After reaching the place Kumāra got a pavilion-of-travel (a camp) to be constructed on the north bank of the Gaṅgā for the stay of Yuan Chwang and himself accompanied by his ministers went to meet Śīlāditya-rāja who, however, on 'seeing him coming was overjoyed, and knowing his respect and love for the Master of Law,[48] ... *did not repeat his former threatening words*'.[49] Thereafter follows the description of Śīlāditya's meeting with Yuan Chwang and their conversation and finally the decision to hold a grand assembly at Kannauj especially to discuss philosophico-religious matters and to establish the correctness of the Chinese guest's views[50] to be followed by another regular quinquennial assembly at Prayāga in both of which all the three participated. According to the *Life*, in the special assembly at Kannauj Bhāskaravarman acted as Brahmā waving a chowrie while Śīlāditya dressed as Śakra held an umbrella over the image of the Buddha in the procession flanking it on the left and right respectively. In the other assembly (at Prayāga) he occupied the south side of the river Yamunā.[51]

The latter part of the episode concerning Bhāskaravarman, Yuan Chwang and Harsha coupled with the fact that Bhāskaravarman had taken the initiative in seeking Harsha's alliance as a measure of caution and safety against the Gauḍa king Śaśāṅka and certain statements of Yuan Chwang and Hwui Li leave no room for doubt that the Kāmarūpa king, theoretically independent though, was a subordinate ally of the Kannauj emperor. One need not be surprised at this apparently contradictory position as it is quite normal in the alliance of two unequal powers. We have already referred to his becoming ***'alarmed'*** and ***'submissive'*** on receiving Śīlāditya's reply asking him to send his head. Then, Yuan Chwang speaks of Śīlāditya as ***'sovereign'***,[52] whereas Kumāra is only spoken of as ***'king.'*** Added to it very significantly, his biographer informs us that 'as Śīlāditya-rāja marched, he was always accompanied by several hundred persons with golden drums, who beat one stroke for every step taken; they called these the "music-pace-drums" (*tsieh-po-lo*). ***Śīlāditya alone used this method; other kings were not permitted to adopt it.***'[53]

Reference must in this connection be made to the statement of Bāṇa that Harsha had anointed a certain Kumāra (*atra devena abhishiktaḥ Kumāraḥ*). In view of the fact that Bāṇa knew Kumāra to be the more popular name of Bhāskara and that no other king bearing this name is known to him[54] the averment, though somewhat exaggerated, indubitably shows that Bāṇa regarded Bhāskara as a vassal of Harsha.[55] Support for it may also be found in the fact that Bhāskara had sent as the most valuable present to Harsha his hereditary umbrella, an insignia of royalty in those days, given by god Varuṇa which had come to him as a family heirloom from very ancient times.[55a] This attitude of Bāṇa is comparable to the descriptions of Yuan Chwang and Hwui Li in respect of Bhāskaravarman *versus* Śīlabhadra and Bhāskaravarman *versus* Śīlāditya and is to be taken with a pinch of salt, and not as literally true.

BHĀSKARA'S INTEREST IN CHINA

Bhāskaravarman was keenly interested in having closer relations with China, and this desire was sharpened by his contact with the Chinese pilgrim. He had a faint idea of Chinese philosophers and Chinese music earlier. When Yuan Chwang visited him at last, he told him - 'At present in various states of India a song has been heard for some time called "the Music of the conquests of Ch'in (Tsin) Wang" of Mahāchīna - this refers to Your Reverence's native country - I presume.' The pilgrim replied -'Yes, this song praises my sovereign's excellences.'[56] It is found elaborated in the *Life* where the same question is said to have been put to him by Śīlāditya in response to which he said, 'In my country when there is a man observable for his quality of protecting the good, capable of averting evil from the people, and able to nourish and cherish with fostering care all living things - then they sound him praise in songs and chants arranged to music, in the first place, for ancestral temple; then for the use of the distant village folk. The king of Ts'in is the same, now, as the reigning Emperor of China - but before the highest authority of the Emperor (*i.e. She-wong-ti*) was established, then he was but invested as prince of Ts'in. This was a period of of disaster in heaven and earth; the people had no ruler, and fields and plains were covered with the bodies of men, and the streams and valleys were full of their blood; during the night ill-omened stars shed their pestilent light, vapours rose with the day, the three rivers were infested by voracious toll-collections, and the four seas were afflicted with the poison of monstrous snakes. The Prince, as the next of kin to the supreme ruler (*ti*), obedient to the call of Heaven, filled with noble ardour, rallied his troops, put down the oppressors (male and female, *k'ing i*) by force; seizing the battle-axe and lance, he quickly calmed the sea, the villagers were profoundly quiet, and the districts resorted to order as before. The sun and moon and stars shone out again, and the world was filled with gratitude for his care. For this reason we sing his praises.'[57]

The musical composition under reference was known in China as the *Ch'in-wang-p'o-ch'en-yao* or 'the music of Ch'in-wang's victory', and its origin is as under: In AD 619 T'ang Kao Tsu's second son Ch'in-wang or Prince of Ch'in named Shih-min succeeded in suppressing the serious rebellion of Liu-wu-chow who ultimately fell into the hands of the Turks who killed him. To commemorate this brilliant military achievement of Ch'in-wang in suppressing this rebellion his soldiers got up a musical performance with song and dance. This performance was named 'Ch'in-wang-p'o-ch'en-yao' or 'Shen-kung-p'o-ch'en-yao' but it was generally called by its short name 'P'o-ch'en-yao'. The dance or posture-making performance was known as 'Ch'i-te-wu' or 'the Dance of Seven Vultures', the name containing a classical allusion. The dance was performed by a troupe of 128 men attired in silver hauberks and armed with spears. The emperor Kao Tsu ordered that the 'P'o-ch'en-yao' should be given when a victorious general returning from a successful campaign entered the capital. At the banquet hosted by T'ai-Tsung, formerly Ch'in-wang, on his accession to the throne this performance, dance and music both, was repeated.[58] It had become so very famous as to reach the various states of India and to form the subject of an inquiry of the two most enlightened Indian rulers of the time.

Chinese philosophy also was a source of attraction to Bhāskaravarman. He was eager to learn more about the doctrines of the well-known Chinese philosopher Lao-tzu who lived about 600 BC and propounded what is commonly known as Taoism, the word *tao* meaning 'the way'. It came into close contact with Buddhism which entered China somewhat later. The mystic doctrines of Lao-tzu were already known to Indians through another Chinese pilgrim Song-yun who had been to India about AD 520 and had discoursed on them and their great expositor Chuang-tzu (fourth century BC) to the king of Udyāna in the Uttarāpatha division of Bhāratavarsha (now in Pakistan). Through these sources and probably through contact with Yuan Chwang who stayed with him for some time Bhāskara's curiosity about Lao-tzu's work was aroused and later he requested the Chinese envoy Li Yi-piao to have the work translated into Sanskrit and sent to him. And attempts at its Sanskrit rendering were reportedly made.[59] This would probably show that Bhāskaravarman had a good knowledge of philosophy and had sufficient grounding in Sanskrit to be able to follow the Sanskrit translation of the philosophical text of Lao-tzu which would have required a sound understanding of both the language and phiosophy.

Kāmarūpa: Yuan Chwang's Account

Yuan Chwang has left a description of Kāmarūpa which is quite revealing in certain respects. Its salient features are as follows:

> It was over 900 *li* to the east of Pun-na-fa-tan-na (Puṇḍravardhana) and was reached after crossing a large river. It was more than a myriad *li* in circuit, and its capital above thirty *li*. The country was low and moist, the crops were regular, the jack-fruit and cocoa were in great esteem though plentiful, there were continuous streams and tanks to the towns, the climate was genial. The people were of honest ways, small of stature and black-looking, their speech differed a little from that of 'Mid-India', they were of violent disposition, and were persevering students, they worshipped the *devas*, and ***did not believe in Buddhism. So there had never been a Buddhist monastery in the land, and whatever Buddhists there were in it performed their acts of devotion secretly***, the *Deva*-temples were some hundreds in number, and the various systems had some myriads of professed adherents. The **reigning king, who was a brahmin by caste, and a descendant of Nārāyaṇa Deva**, was named Bhāskaravarman ('Sun-armour'), his other name being Kumāra ('Youth'), *the sovereignty had been transmitted in the family for 1000 generations.* His Majesty was a lover of learning and his subjects followed his example,

> *men of ability came from far lands to study here,* ***though the king was not a Buddhist, he treated accomplished śramaṇas with respect.***[60]

He also informs us that the country east of Kāmarūpa was a series of hills and hillocks without any principal city, and it reached to the south-west barbarians [of China], hence the inhabitants were akin to the Man and Lao. He learned from the people [of Kāmarūpa] that the south-west borders of Szuchuan were distant about two months' journey, but the mountains and rivers were hard to pass, there were pestilential vapours and poisonous snakes and herbs. In the south-east of the country [viz. Kāmarūpa] were wild elephants which ravaged in herds, and so there was a good supply of elephants for war purposes.[61]

Bhāskara and Wang-hiwen-tse's Mission

We come to know of another, rather curious, facet of Bhāskaravarman's activities in connection with the mission of the Chinese envoy Wang-hiwen-tse following Harsha Śīlāditya's death. We learn from the Chinese sources that in the twentieth year of the Ching-kwan period, viz. AD 646, the Chinese emperor despatched Wang-hiwen-tse under the title of Yeu-weī-so-fu-chang-shi accompanied by General Tsiang-shi-jin to the kingdom of Magadha only to find at arrival that king Śīlāditya was already dead and his kingdom, which had fallen into a state of anarchy, was usurped by one of his ministers whose name has been transliterated into Chinese as Na-fo-ti-a-la-na-shun.[62] On knowing of the arrival of the Chinese mission the usurper sent soldiers to oppose it and was successful owing to the mission having only a few dozens of cavaliers and used violence to make other kingdoms pay him tribute. But Hiwen-tse resolved to retaliate and with substantial armed contingents provided by some neighbouring powers general Tsiang-shi-jin was able not only to defeat the rebel minister but also to behead thousands of soldiers and also capture his queen (who encouraged people to oppose the Chinese general) and several thousands of men and women and some twenty thousand cattle-heads. ***Among the kings who helped the Chinese was included Shi-kieu-ma (Śrīkumāra ?), 'king of eastern India'***, who supplied 'thirty thousand oxen and horses and provisions for the entire army and weapons including bows, scimitars and collars of great value.' 'The king of Kia-mo-lo' (Kāmarūpa) also gave the Chinese general some rare articles including ***a map of his states***[62a] and several statuettes of Lao-tsu.[63] However, in the absence of any independent corroborative evidence it is just impossible to judge the veracity of this account which looks more like a highly exaggerated fiction than history. In case it is even slightly correct and the Kāmarūpa king Bhāskaravarman did really play some role in the expedition, it would only serve to indicate that he lacked patriotism and also could not quite understand the military implications of maps, for otherwise he would not have passed them over to the Chinese howsoever friendly they might have been at the moment. It is likely that this episode landed him in the imbroglio of an unexpected calamity. The Tibetan monarch Sroṅ-bstān-sgam-po (died AD 650), who also reportedly assisted the Chinese, invaded and conquered Assam.[64] According to some historians, this was probably the reason for the sudden end of the Bhauma-Nāraka dynasty beginning with Pushyavarman after its most powerful ruler Bhāskaravarman.[65] However, as of now there is nothing to verify these traditions.

A Possible Reference in Dāmodaragupta's *Kuṭṭanī-mata*

Verse 651 of the erotico-didactic poem *Kuṭṭanī-mata* of the Kashmiri poet-politician Dāmodaragupta (end-eighth–early ninth centuries AD)[66] may perhaps contain information about an interesting episode in the life of Bhāskaravarman in case it is treated as historical. The stanza under reference tells us that when Bhāskaravarman went to the divine abode (i.e. passed away), he was accompanied on the funeral pyre by his beloved who was unable to bear the pangs of separation from her lover even though she was dissuaded from doing so by the king.[67] That Dāmodaragupta intended to represent Bhāskaravarman as a monarch is vouched for by the reported intervention of a king who was evidently his successor. The identification of this Bhāskaravarman, however, poses a serious problem which defies a definite solution in the present state of inadequate information. It is pertinent to mention in this context that the poet has named a number of personages to illustrate the treacherous character of a procuress (verses 35-38), the selfless love of a hetaira (verses 559-66) and the like.[68] But most of them are undoubtedly fictitious figures invented to exemplify the various aspects of a prostitute's craft. Likewise, the Bhāskaravarman under reference, too, may have been a purely imaginary figure. And even if one were to regard him as a historical personage, it is not easy to identify him. The only Bhāskaravarman known to sober history is the homonymous king of Kāmarūpa who was, as we have seen, an illustrious contemporary of Harshavardhana Śīlāditya and Yuan Chwang. There is nothing improbable in Dāmodaragupta having heard of king Bhāskaravarman, especially as he shows full awareness of Harsha and his times.[69] And that our poet was not averse to history is amply borne out by his valuable allusions to the Kalachuri king Anaṅgaharsha which we have discussed elsewhere.[70] And if the two Bhāskaravarmans are regarded as the same, this allusion will supply a highly interesting piece of information about the Kāmarūpa king under discussion not available from any other source. But in the absence of an independent corroborative evidence on the point, the question is better left open.[71]

Kumāra Bhāskaravarman's Presents to Harsha

The account of the precious presents sent by Bhāskaravarman to Harsha through his envoy Haṁsavega along with his offer of undying friendship met with in Bāṇa's *Harsha-charita* (VII Uchchhvāsa)[72] is pregnant with great interest and value inasmuch as it gives an idea of the economic products of Kāmarūpa during the seventh century AD traditions of which, of course, must go back to a considerably earlier period. We may therefore refer to them in brief in these pages.

1. The first and foremost was an exceptionally large wonderful snow-white silk umbrella of Varuṇa known as Ābhoga which had come down to him as family heirloom and possessed numerous mythical properties and effects. This umbrella with its miraculous qualities is also mentioned in a Kashmir chronicle in connection with the marriage of the Prāgjyotisha princess Amṛitaprabhā with prince Meghavāhana.[73] It had on top the figure of a swan with its wings spread out and was decked all-round with multitudes of knitted pearls from which were suspended minute chowries. Harsha was amazed to see such a precious present.
2. Ornaments with various devices embossed and coming down in the family from the time of Bhagadatta, etc., and believed to be the special favour of the progenitor of the lineage.
3. Crest-jewels.
4. Several varieties of white necklaces.
5. Varieties of white silks rolled round (*thāns*) and kept in cane-baskets of various shades. They could bear washing.
6. Goblets for drinking wines made of oyster-shells, conch-shells, crystal or lapis lazuli (*galvarka*), etc., adorned by skilful artists with beautifully embossed designs.
7. Shields kept in sheaths to preserve their sheen and decked with beautiful gold-work made from black leather brought from Kārdaraṅga[74] island.
8. Waist-belts as soft as the birch-bark sheets.[75]
9. Pillows of the soft leather of the *samūraka* deer[76] and of smooth figured textures.
10. Seats of cane with slight reddish yellow tinge resembling the fresh sprout of the *priyaṅgu* tree.
11. Books containing excellent sayings (*subhāshitas*) and made of the aloe bark and resembling in hue the ripe pink cucumber.
12. Luscious milky betel-nut fruits hanging from their sprays and green like young *harita* doves and reddish like ripe *paṭola* (a specie of cucumber) from which the juice was flowing.
13. Thick bamboo-tubes full of mango-juice and covered with the sheaths of the *kapotikā* and *palāśa* leaves with the hue of the cheeks of an angry ape (slightly reddish).
14. Similar tubes filled with the oil of black aloe.
15. Black aloe of the dark hue resembling pounded collyrium contained in gunny bags.[77]
16. The *gośīrsha* variety of sandal-wood giving relief from summer-heat.[78]

17. Crystals of camphor, cool and pure, and as white as bits of ice.
18. Bags of musk oxen (*kastūrikā*).
19. Leaves of *kakkola* with hanging ripe *kakkola* fruits.[79]
20. Bunches of clove-flowers.[80]
21. Clusters of nutmeg.
22. Jars covered with cloth containing sweet wine whose sweet smell was writ in the air.[81]
23. Multitudes of *chāmaras*, both white and black.
24. Pairs of painting-panels carved from inside and from which were suspended painting-brushes and small bottle-gourds containing colours for painting.[82]
25. Pairs of *kinnaras,* orang-outangs (*vana-mānushas*), *jīvañjīvakas* (a specie of birds) and mermen (*jala-mānushas*) with their necks tied with golden chains.
26. Kastūrikā specie of deer filling the atmosphere with fragrance.
27. Domesticated female *chamarī* deer (yak cows).
28. Parrots, *śārikās* and other birds in gold-painted bamboo-cages reciting several kinds of good sayings (which they had evidently simulated from human beings).
29. *Chakora* birds in cages of crystal.
30. Earrings of ivory studded with the multitudes of pearls drawn from the heads of *jala-hastins* (water-elephants).[83]

All these were not isolated single objects but their heaps and quantities were presented which serves as a running commentary on the highly developed craftsmanship as well as products and trade of the North-East in the seventh century AD. It is interesting to note in this context that while some of these items are still well-known products of the region, many of these articles came to North-East India from some other countries in Asia, more particularly from South-East Asia which was then known as Dvīpāntara. This would show that Prāgjyotisha had close commercial contacts with these regions from which it imported large volumes of commodities in demand evidently in exchange for the items it exported to them. Obviously, Prāgjyotisha had close prosperous commercial relations with the rest of India as well as with the outside world. The reference to a large volume of aloe sheets containing *subhāshitas* is of particular interest inasmuch as it shows that Prāgjyotisha in general and Kāmarūpa in particular had already turned into great literary centres of Sanskrit.

2. WAS AVANTIVARMAN AN IMMEDIATE SUCCESSOR OF BHĀSKARAVARMAN ?

Bhāskaravarman's eventful reign came to a sudden close around mid-seventh century AD, a precise date for this happening being in the present state of our information just indeterminable. The only thing that may be averred precisely is that it occurred after the mission of Wang-hiwen-tse in AD 647-48. What happened to the vast kingdom inherited from his predecessors and further enlarged by Bhāskara also is not known. Perhaps he, like his illustrious ally Harsha Śīlāditya, passed away without leaving a male issue to succeed him. And shortly after, about AD 650-51, we find a certain Sālastambha on the throne of Kāmarūpa.

Some scholars, however, think that a king named Avantivarman mentioned in some versions of the concluding stanza (*bharata-vākya*) of the famous Sanskrit political drama *Mudrā-Rākshasa* of Viśākhadatta was the immediate successor of Bhāskaravarman. The stanza in question, according to this recension, expresses the wish that King Avantivarman, assisted by his prosperous relations and servants, may protect for long the earth which was rescued after the deluge by god Vishṇu in his Varāha (Boar) form with the forepart of his teeth which was now being frightened by the Mlechchhas.[84] The monarch is represented as the manifestation of that self-existent God to whose arms the earth goddess now clings because of the fear from the Mlechchhas.

The reason for the association of Avantivarman with Bhāskaravarman's lineage is the use of the expression *pārthiva* ('son of *pṛithivī*', viz. 'earth') in the sense of 'king' and the reference to the Varāha manifestation of god Vishṇu from the union of whom the Bhauma-Nāraka dynasty to which Bhāskaravarman belonged traced its origin. The play, according to its prologomena, was composed by the poet Viśākhadatta who was the son of one Pṛithu, styled *Mahārāja*, and grandson of the *Sāmanta* (feudal chief) named Vaṭeśvaradatta.[85]

Ghosh J.C. was the first to offer this suggestion,[86] and thereafter it has found numerous champions, some of them even more vociferous than its original proponent. Ghosh felt that Viśākhadatta flourished towards the close of the seventh century AD and belonged to Kāmarūpa and conjectured that Avantivarman was the son of Bhāskaravarman. This conjecture was supported by Barua K.L. who pointed out that the danger of the Mlechchha rebellion was actually imminent in Kāmarūpa at that time as the strong rule of Bhāskaravarman ended with his death and after the rule, lasting not more than five years, of Avantivarman (*c.* AD 650-55) we find the Mlechchha king Sālastambha wielding power.[87] He was further in concurrence with the view of Vasu N.N that Jayatuṅgavarman, mentioned as the overlord of Lokanātha known from his Tipperāh charter, was Bhāskaravarman's immediate successor[88] whom he further proposed to equate with Avantivarman.[89] R.M. Nath too, supports the identification of Avantivarman as the immediate successor of Bhaskaravarman and holds that he was overthrown by Sālastambha.[90] D.R. Bhandarkar feels that Devavarman referred to by the Chinese traveller I-tsing as the King of Eastern India may have been a king of Kāmarūpa and probably Bhāskara's son.[91] P.C. Choudhury gives the question a new dimension by supposing that Devavarman of I-tsing is an inversion of 'Varmadeva' taken by the rulers of the Varman line as well as by some other later Kāmarūpa rulers and in that case he may be identified with Viśākhadatta's Avantivarman.[92] He further equates the two with Sālastambha and tries to strengthen Ghosh's theory identifying Viśākhadatta's Avantivarman as the immediate successor of Bhāskaravarman and holds that Viśākhadatta was most probably his contemporary.[93] The strongest champion of this theory is, however, Sharma M.M. who has tried to justify it on some additional considerations.[94] These include, *inter alia*, the following:

1. The *Mudrā-Rākshasa* was composed in North Bengal which then formed part of Kāmarūpa and it refers to some tribes of the North-East like the Khasas or Khāsīs;
2. the name Avantivarman is similar to those of Bhāskaravarman and his predecessors;
3. the epithet *pārthiva*, 'son of Pṛithivī', refers to the origin of the Varmans from the earth goddess;
4. most of the copperplate charters of the Kāmarūpa kings contain an invariable allusion to Vishṇu's Varāha manifestation; and
5. most of the official records of the Kāmarūpa monarchs, and especially the two known grants of Bhāskaravarman, like the *Mudrā-Rākshasa*, have a *maṅgala* stanza invoking Śiva.

We feel, however, that none of these arguments is conclusive enough to establish the contention, and these are very general points that neither prove nor disprove the suggested identification.

As against this, there is sufficient ground to dismiss the theory. First of all, there are variant readings of the king's name, viz. Chandragupta, Avantivarman, Dantivarman and Rantivarman, the last reading being meaningless and discardable. Of the remaining three names, as shown by Hillebrandt, Avantivarman and Dantivarman are later emendations and thus Chandragupta appears to be the most likely one, though there can be no finality in this matter. However, even if, just for argument's sake, one were to accept the reading Avantivarman as the only one, there is no guarantee that he belonged to Kāmarūpa alone because we have as yet no record mentioning Avantivarman as a king of Kāmarūpa. As against it, we know of a ruler of Kashmir and a Maukhari king of this name from reliable historical records. Then, there is nothing to suggest that the author belonged to Kāmarūpa or, for that matter, to any other region, and we can only say that he belonged to India. And this Viśākhadatta appears to be the same as Viśākhadeva, the author of another political play, *Devī-Chandragupta*, of which only fragments have been located from some later works. These are the only two well-known plays of the same genre and appear to proceed from the same pen. Though the age of the author has been conceived variously by different critics, it looks more likely that he was the court-poet of the Gupta emperor Chandra Gupta II Vikramāditya.[95] Then, the word *pārthiva*, though literally capable of meaning 'son of Pṛithivī' as thought by some, is much more commonly used just in the sense of 'king', and the reference to the rescue of the earth by Vishṇu in his boar manifestation is too common and met with in several inscriptions to justify its exclusive association with Kāmarūpa. As we have just stated, there is nothing whatever to determine the region where Viśākhadatta flourished, and to connect him with some of the brāhmaṇa donees of the Nidhānpur plates of Bhāskaravarman, as some have attempted, is also without any basis except that they have *datta*-ending names. And there is nothing to show that they reached the status of *sāmanta* or *mahārāja* as the author was. So we may dismiss the theory without any further discussion as purely imaginary.[96]

3. BHAUMA-KARAS OF ORISSA, AN OFFSHOOT OF THE BHAUMA-NĀRAKAS OF KĀMARŪPA

From about the eighth century AD, a dynasty called Bhauma-Kara ruled over the northern part of Orissa. Its origin is, however, shrouded in mystery. But the official records of the family claim that it hailed from the Bhauma lineage like the Bhauma-Nāraka kings of Kāmarūpa. Thus, the earliest known record of the family, viz. the Neulpur plate of Śubhākara, refers to Kshemaṅkara, the founder of the line, as born from the Bhauma line.[97] This statement is repeated in several other grants of the members of the dynasty including the Chītalpur plate of Śubhākara[98] and the Chaurāshī plate of Śivakara II.[99] From these allusions it is clear that this dynasty also claimed origin from the Bhauma line which reflects the belief in its original progenitor (not the founder of the dynasty) being born of Bhūmi or the 'earth.' Basing on the description of Kshemaṅkara as born of the Bhauma line, R.D. Banerji suggested long back that the Bhauma-Karas most probably traced their descent from Naraka, supposed to have been the son of the earth, like the kings of Kāmarūpa.[100] The Chaurāshī plate of Śivakara describes the benefactor as a descendant of the Utkala-*kula* of the Bhaumas.[101] The Tālcher plate of Śubhākara speaks of the donor as a descendant of, *inter alia*, Bhagadatta,[102] who was also the first traditional king of the Bhaumas of Kāmarūpa. All these should leave no doubt that the Bhauma-Karas of Utkala regarded their dynasty as originating from the earth and Bhagadatta, who was the son of Naraka who himself was believed to have been born of the earth (*bhūmi*) through her union with god Vishṇu in his Varāha (Boar) manifestation.[103]

We also have some clue to find out as to how and when the Utkala branch of the Bhauma lineage came into being. The Kāṭhmāṇḍū Paśupatinātha temple inscription of the Nepal king Jayadeva Parachakrakāma[104] informs us that he married Rājyamatī, daughter of Harshadeva, who was the lord of Gauḍa, Uḍra, Kaliṅga, etc. Rājyamatī is further said to have been born in the lineage of Bhagadatta.[105] In view of the latter statement her father Harshadeva has been identified, probably rightly, with Harshavarman who flourished about mid-eighth century AD. This is about the time when the Bhauma-Kara dynasty came into existence in Orissa. It appears likely that Harshadeva conquered Uḍra during the lifetime of his father Vajradeva and that the Nepalese *praśasti-kāra* credited it to the account of his patron's father-in-law. And one of the generals or officers left out in the newly conquered territory founded the Bhauma-Kara kingdom. Thus, there is no doubt whatsoever that the Bhauma-Karas of Orissa owed their origin to the Bhauma-Nārakas of Kāmarūpa.

4. SUMMING UP

We have illustrated above that ancient Prāgjyotisha or the North-East had very intimate relations with the rest of India of which it was an integral component, geographically and culturally, despite its own distinctive culture and physical elements as in the case of the other regions of India. Like them, it also contributed lion's share to the prosperity and growth of Indian culture. In subsequent period also it continued on the same track, and we know of numerous brāhmaṇas immigrating to Prāgjyotisha from other parts of India and being patronised by its rulers and Kāmarūpa brāhmaṇas going over to and settling in other areas. We have to restrict ourselves to brāhmaṇas as we have only their activities recorded. And they undoubtedly carried and transmitted strong cultural elements to wherever they went.

NOTES AND REFERENCES

1. *Prāgjyotish-endreṇa Kumāreṇa prahito Haṁsavega-nāmā dūto...*
   Harsha-charita, Uchchhvāsa, VII, p. 288.
2. *Haṁsavega, śrīmān kachchit kuśalī Kumāraḥ.*
   Ibid. p. 289.
3. *Bhadra.... asya Kumārāl=lābho na vismayāya.*
   Ibid., p. 293.
4. *Tat tathā yatetha yathā na chiram iyam asmān kleśayati Kumāra-darśan-otkaṇṭhā.*
   Ibid., p. 296.
5. *Bhāskara-dyutir—Bhāskaravarm-āpara-nāmā.*
   Ibid., p. 295.
6. Thomas Watters, *On Yuan Chwang's Travels in India*, I, p. 348.
7. *Ibid*., II, p. 186.
8. *The Life of Hieun-tsiang*, pp. 165, 169, 170, 172, etc.
9. *She-kia-fang-che*, p. 104.
10. M. Pauthier, *op. cit*., p. 20.
11. Strangely enough, his two well-known inscriptions, viz. Dūbī and Nidhānpur plates, and the Nālandā and Dūbī seal inscriptions do not mention the name Kumāra. It may be just casual and some future epigraphical and other finds in Kāmarūpa might throw more light on this problem. But in view of the copious evidence from the *Harsha-charita* and the Chinese sources there ought to be no doubt about both, Kumāra and Bhāskaravarman, being his personal names.
12. *Kāmarūpa-śāsanāvali*, Introduction, pp. 16-18; *EI*, XII, p. 70.
13. *EHK*, pp. 57-58.
14. *HCPA*, pp. 180-81. He thinks that Kumāra was a 'nickname' of Bhāskaravarman.

14a. 'Was Bhāskaravarman a Feudatory?', *Journal of North-East Council of Social Science Research*, XXII, No. II, Oct. 1998, pp. 5-10.

15. For a discussion, see the previous chapter.
16. T. Watters, *op. cit*., II, p. 186.
17. *Kirata-jana-kriti*, pp. 90-91.
18. *CII*, III, p. 203, verses 13-14.
19. This name or style occurs in the Dūbī plates. *Vide* D.C. Sircar, 'Dūbī Plates of Bhāskaravarman', *EI*, XXX, 1953-54, p. 303, verse 63.
20. D.C. Sircar, 'Gauḍa-Kāmarūpa Struggle in the 6th-9th Centuries', *IHQ*, XXVI, 1955, pp. 241-46.
21. R.C. Majumdar in *HCIP*, III: *CA*, p. 92. *HCPA*, pp. 177f.
22. D.C. Sircar in *IHQ*, XXVI, 1955, p. 246; *EI*, XXX, p. 294; *Journal of the Bihar Research Society*, XXXV, pp. 130ff.; Sudhakara Chattopadhyaya, *Early History of Northern India*, pp. 279-80.
23. Had he defeated Supratishṭhitavarman and Bhāskaravarman, this feat also, like that in the case of their father, must have been specified in the aforesaid Aphsad inscription.
24. See the description of his brother-in-law Grahavarman's murder and his own resolve to uproot the Gauḍas.

25. *Harsha-charita,* Uchchhvāsa VII.
25a. The author of the *Ārya-mañjuśrī-mūla-kalpa* mentions often important historical personages by the first letter of their names which more often than not has resulted in protracted controversies regarding their equations.
25b. The text often employs synonyms for the names of individuals which have occasioned debates about their identities.
26. See K.P. Jayaswal, *An Imperial History of India*, p. 50, text, pp. 53-54, lines 721-26.
27. J.F. Fleet, *CII*, III, p. 284.
28. N.R. Ray, 'Harsha-Śīlāditya: A Revised Study', *IHQ*, III, 1927, p.775; R.G. Basak, *History of North-Eastern India*, p. 152; Sudhakara Chattopadhyaya, *op. cit.*, p. 278. The seal-matrix is generally referred to an early phase of Śaśāṅka's career and taken to indicate that he commenced his political career as a feudatory chief. *Vide* R.C. Majumdar (ed.), *History of Bengal,* I, p. 59; B.P. Sinha, *The Decline of the Kingdom of Magadha*, pp. 222-23. The suggestion of S. Chattopadhyaya (*op. cit.*, p. 280) that the absence of the imperial style *mahārājādhirāja* in the two Midnāpur plates of Śaśāṅka (R.C. Majumdar, 'Two Copper Plates of Śaśāṅka from Midnapore', *JRASBL*, XI [1945], pp. 1-9) indicates that they, too, were issued after Śaśāṅka had become a vassal fails to carry conviction. The charters were composed in verse which made it impossible to mention the imperial style and therefore it by itself is of no historical significance.
29. E. Hultzsch, 'Plates of the Time of Śaśāṅkarāja, Gupta Saṁvat 300', *EI*, VI, pp. 143-46.
30. P. 57.
31. Mādhavarāja II Sainyabhīta's charters, dating from his 13th year onward, were issued without any reference to his former suzerain and record his performance of Aśvamedha and other Śrauta sacrifices. Even if we were to assume that he began to rule in AD 619, which is his first known date, his 13th year could not have fallen later than AD 631.
32. Jayaswal, *op. cit.*, p. 50, verse 732.
33. *EI*, XII, pp. 65-69; XIX, pp. 115ff.; 245ff.
34. Practically the same view is held by P. Bhattacharya (*EI*, XII, 65f.; *IA*, XLIII, pp. 95ff.; *Kāmarūpa-śāsanavali*, p. 5), R.S. Tripathi (*History of Kaunauj*, p. 103) and D.C. Sircar (*IHQ*, XIX, 1943 pp. 287ff). (It is a review of Hirananda Sastri's *Nalanda and its Epigraphical Material*).
35. This is based on the place of issue of his Nidhānpur charter. It is equally likely, however, that the charter was issued from Karṇasuvarṇa merely to commemorate the triumphant entry of Bhāskaravarman into the metropolis of his dreaded enemy, Śaśāṅka, who had earlier defeated him and his elder brother and taken both as prisoners of war. It is interesting to note in this connection that the lands granted through this charter were situated about modern Pañchakhaṇḍa division of the Sylhet district of Bangladesh, and not in Gauḍa, the erstwhile kingdom of Śaśāṅka. See the discussion in the previous chapter. Also *vide IHQ*, VII, pp. 743-46; Jogendra Chandra Ghosh, 'Donated Land of the Nidhānpur Charter of Bhāskaravarman of Kāmarūpa',

IC, II, 1935, pp. 153-57; *IA*, LXI, p. 44.

36. For other views on the question, see D.C. Ganguly, 'Political Condition of Bengal during Hiuen-tsang's Visit', *IHQ*, XV, 1939, pp. 122-24; B.K. Barua, *CHA*, pp. 24ff.; R.G. Basak, *op. cit.*, 228-29; K.L. Barua, *EHK*, pp. 56f.; Sudhakara Chattopadhyaya, *op. cit.*, p. 305, etc.
37. In the seal-inscriptions of Bhāskaravarman his earliest recorded royal ancestor Pushyavarman is styled *Prāgjyotish-eśvara*. *Vide* the previous chapter.
38. *EI*, XXVII, 1947-48, p. 18.
39. Watters, *op. cit.*, II, p. 186.
40. P. 169 where he is referred to as 'Kumāra-rāja of Eastern India'.
41. *The Life*, p. 188. See also S. Beal's Introduction, pp. xxvi-xxvii, where some important details about the use and control of this route are given.
42. The Chinese text *Ma-twa-lin* refers to Shi-kieu-ma (Śrī-Kumāra ?) as the 'King of Eastern India'. See M. Pauthier, *op. cit.*, p. 20.
43. Watters, *op. cit.*, II, p.186.
44. *Ibid.*
45. *Life*, pp. 166-71. He also narrates how it was predicted by a Nirgrantha (Jaina) astrologer.
46. Watters, *op. cit.*, I, pp. 348-49.
47. *Life*, p. 172. The statement of Hwui Li that Bhāskara went to Kajaṅgala to meet Harsha along with Yuan Chwang and a huge armada passing along the Gaṅgā has been taken by some scholars to prove Bhāskara's control over Bengal during the lifetime of Harsha. See D.C. Ganguly in *IHQ*, XV, 1939, pp. 122ff.; R.C. Majumdar in *HCPI*, III: *CA*, pp. 139-41. However, this by itself is quite inadequate to establish this hypothesis. For, Bhāskara being an esteemed ally of Harsha and going to meet him at his bidding could certainly pass through this territory even if it was in Harsha's possession.
48. This is how Yuan Chwang is called by Hwui Li.
49. *Ibid.*
50. It was especially convened because of Yuan Chwang and was in the nature of intellectual debates (*śāstrārthas*) very popular in those days. But the account is greatly biased in favour of the Chinese pilgrim and has in consequence turned utterly unreliable.
51. The accounts of both these gatherings are highly bloated in the Chinese sources, more especially by Shaman Hwui Li, and one has perforce to read between the lines.
52. Watters, I, p. 349.
53. *Life*, p. 173. Stress conveyed through bold and italicised type is ours.
54. The view of R.S. Tripathi (*op. cit.*, p. 105) and D.C. Sircar (*IHQ*, XIX, 1943) that this refers to the appointment of Mādhavagupta of the Later Gupta family in Magadha has nothing to commend itself, as he is not called Kumāra anywhere in the family's records.
55. For a similar view, see Jai Prakash Singh, *op, cit.* Of course, it is difficult to concede his position that Bhāskaravarman had formally accepted Harsha's suzerainty in view of the express statement of Haṁsavega that his master was determined not to bow before any one except god Śiva and Harsha's

response as reported by Bāṇa himself.

55a. *HC*, pp. 289-90 and the description of Bhāskara's presents to Harsha sent through his messenger Haṁsavega in the sequel.

56. Watters, *op. cit.*, I, p. 348.

57. *Life*, pp. 174-75.

58. Watters, I, pp. 349-50. It is quite likely, as suggested by S.K. Chatterjee, that it is not the song itself but its tune that may have come to be known to the Indians. It is quite obvious for it would have been very difficult to understand the Chinese language even for the elite.

59. S.K. Chatterjee, *Kirāta-jana-kṛiti*, pp. 93-94.

60. Watters, *op. cit.*, II, pp. 185-86. Interesting portions of this account have been italicised and boldened by us for inviting scholarly attention.

61. *Ibid.*, p. 186.

62. The Indian transliteration of the Chinese name is difficult. The translator in French, M. Julien, has not given the name's full Indian equivalent but begins it with *Nava*. But it could have been 'Navātyarjuna,' 'a modern one who had surpassed Arjuna'.

62a. This is a very valuable information indicating as it does that ancient Indians had made good progress in cartographic science.

63. M. Pauthier, *op. cit.*, p. 20. *Vide* also *Journal Asiatique*, 1900, pp. 297ff.; P.C. Bagchi, *Sino-Indian Studies*, I, p. 69. For a general account of the event, see *HCPI*, III: *CA*, pp. 124-26.

64. S. Lévi, *Le Nepal*, II, p. 148.

65. *Vide HCIP*, III: *CA*, p. 141.

66. For the historical data of the work supporting this date, see Ajay Mitra Shastri, *ISKMD*, pp. 6-16. The period of his literary activity lay most probably in the early years of the ninth century AD.

67. *Bhāskaravarmaṇi yāte sura-vasatiṁ vārit-āpi bhūpatinā* I
Tadduḥkham asahamānā praviveśa vilāsinī dahanam II

68. Several men and women are mentioned by name, evidently to impart a semblance of reality, for illustrating the conversation of procuresses, courtesans and their lovers. *Vide* verses 331-67, 743-55, etc. All these as well as Purandara, Sundarasena, Guṇapālita, Hāralatā, Mañjarī, etc., who form the principal characters of the poem, are undoubtedly fictitious figures. But that by itself does not preclude the possibility of some personages being historical.

69. See verses 801-9, 880-929, describing the enactment of the *Ratnāvalī* of Harsha which is quite correct and realistic.

70. For the discussion of the allusion to Anaṅgaharsha, *vide ISKMD*, pp. 10-15.

71. This allusion has engaged the attention of some historians. P.C. Choudhury (*HCPA*, p. 348) regards the identification as extremely doubtful, for Bhāskaravarman, according to him, probably remained a celibate throughout his life. This view is evidently based on Bhāskaravarman's other name Kumāra being taken as a *viruda* or title, which, taken literally, would denote a bachelor, a celibate, an unmarried male. But, as we have seen above, Kumāra was just another and perhaps more popular name of Bhāskaravaman

and not a title as thought by Choudhury. Then, Yuan Chwang, who informs us that Kumāra was another name of Bhāskaravarman, renders it by 'Youth'. B.N. Shastri ('Is Bhāskaravarmā, the King of Kāmarūpa, referred to in the Kuṭṭanī-mata of Dāmodaragupta ?', *Summaries of Papers,* All-India Oriental Conference, XXIII Session, p. 117) concludes that Bhāskaravarman of the *Kuṭṭanī-mata* is not a historical figure.

72. For the original, see *Harsha-charita,* pp. 289-93.

73. That this parasol had been famous even earlier is vouched for by Kalhaṇa (*Rāja-taraṅgiṇī,* II. 148-50) who narrates how the shade of the parasol of Varuṇa fell on the prince Meghavāhana who went to participate in the *svayaṁvara* of the Prāgjyotisha princess Amṛitaprabhā whose choice fell on him. We are further told that this parasol was snatched from Varuṇa by king Naraka who had carried it away and in due course it turned into his family's heirloom. It was believed that it cast its shade on no one but a sovereign of the whole globe (*chakravartin*). The original runs as under:

तत्र तं वारुणं छत्रं छायया राजसन्निधौ।
भेजे वरस्रजा राजकन्यका चामृतप्रभा।।१४८।।
राज्ञा हि नरकेणैतद् वरुणादुष्णवारणम्।
आनीतमकरोच्छायां न विना चक्रवर्तिनम्।।१५०।।

As we have seen in the previous chapter, Meghavāhana and Amṛitaprabhā flourished about mid-fifth century AD.

74. The island of Kārdaraṅga was also known as Karmaraṅga or Charmaraṅga and formed a part of the Malay Archipelago . *Vide* V.S. Agrawala, *HCESA,* p. 168.

75. According to V.S. Agrawala (*ibid.*), *jātī-paṭṭikās* were rolled bundles of the *mūṁgā* silk which bore the designs of *jāti* flowers. The commentator Śaṅkara, however, regards them as fine waist-belts.

76. Agrawala (*ibid.*), however, thinks that these pillows were stuffed with the hair of the *samūra* deer or birds and that these were made of silken cloth which was woven with foliage patterns and other designs.

77. F.W. Thomas (*Harsha-charita*, Engl. translation, pp. 213ff.) has taken *paṭṭa-sūtra-prasevaka* of the original to mean 'sacks of woven silk', whereas it appears to refer to the gunny bags.

78. The *gośīrsha* variety of sandal-wood was brought from the Timore island in the eastern group of islands as shown by Sylvain Levi. See V.S. Agrawala, *HCESA*, p. 169.

79. *Kakkola* or *Takkola* was probably brought from the homonymous localities of the Malay peninsula and was named after its provenance. It was the chief port of its shipment. See *ibid.* The commentator Śaṅkara splits the word *chollaka* into *cha* and *ullaka* and takes *ullaka* to denote the juice of a fragrant fruit and this meaning is followed by Thomas.

80. According to Kālidāsa (*Raghu-vaṁśa*, VI. 57), the clove trees were brought from the Malay island.

81. *Cholaka-kalaśīḥ* of the original is actually a technical expression which refers to earthen jars (*surāhī*) covered with wet cloth which Thomas has failed to

follow as he was not familiar with this Indian practice.

82. Thomas has not understood the actual connotation of this description and has rendered it merely as 'carved boxes of panels for painting, with brushes and gourds attached.'

83. For a detailed explanatory account of these presents, see V.S. Agrawala, *HCESA,* pp. 167-70.

84. वाराहीमात्मयोनेस्तनुमतनुबलामास्थितस्यानुरूपाम् ।
यस्य प्राग्दन्तकोटिं प्रलयपरिगता शिश्रिये भूतधात्री ।
म्लेच्छैरुद्वीज्यमाना भुजयुगमधुना पीवरं राजमूर्त्तेः
स श्रीमद्बन्धुभृत्यश्चिरमवतु महीं पार्थिवोऽवन्तिवर्मा ।।

Mudrā-Rākshasa, VII. 19.

There are variant readings of the king's name as will be pointed out in the sequel.

85. अद्य सामन्तवटेश्वरदत्तपौत्रस्य महाराजपदभाक्पृथुसूनोः कवेरर्विशाखदत्तस्य कृतिः मुद्राराक्षसं नाम नाटकं नाटयितव्यम् ।

Ibid., Act I, beginning.

86. *JPASB*, XXVI, pp. 241-45.
87. *EHK*, pp. 109-10.
88. *Social History of Kamarupa*, III.
89. 'Kāmarūpa in the Seventh Century AD', *JARS*, I, 1933, pp, 9-103; reproduced in *SEHA*, pp. 14-22.
90. *Background of Assamese Culture*, p. 40.
91. 'A List of Inscriptions of Northern India in Brāhmī and its Derivative Scripts, from about 200 A.C.', Appendix to *EI*, XIX-XXIII, p. 401, fn. 8.
92. *HCPA*, p. 206.
93. N.N. Dasgupta had earlier suggested that Devavarman was a successor of Bhāskaravarman. See 'The Occupation of Bengal by a King of Kāmarūpa', *IC*, II, 1935, pp. 37-45.
94. *IAA,* Introduction, pp. 30-32.
95. S.R. Goyal, *A History of the Imperial Guptas*, pp. 223-24 and fn. 1 at p. 224.
96. D. Sharma has also dismissed this theory. *Vide* his *KŚ*, Part I, pp. 57-58.
97. R.D. Banerji, 'Neulpur Plate of Śubhākara: The 8th Year', *EI*, XV, 1919-20, p. 3, verse 1.
98. Also called Hindon plate after the then state in which the provenance was situated. See Binayak Misra, 'Hindol Plate of Śubhākaradeva', *JBORS*, XVI, 1930, pp. 69-83.
99. Narayan Tripathi, 'Chaurasi Grant of Śivakaradea', *ibid.*, XIV, 1928, pp. 292-306.
100. *EI*, XV, p. 2.
101. *JBORS*, XV, 1928, pp. 292-306.
102. Binayak Misra, *Orissa under the Bhauma-Karas*, pp. 32-39.
103. Several other scholars have also earlier expressed the same view. See R.P. Chanda in *Journal of the Royal Society of Arts*, 1934; K.L. Barua, 'Origin of the Bhauma-Karas of Orissa', *JARS*, II, 1935, p. 106 (reproduced in *SEHA*, pp. 65-

66); D.R. Bhandarkar, 'A List of the Inscriptions of Northern India in Brāhmī and its Derivative Scripts, from about 200 A. C.', Appendix to *EI*, XIX-XXIII, p. 380, fn. 1. However, there are others who do not agree with this view and instead trace their origin from some local tribes. For a summary of all these views, see Umakanta Subuddhi, *The Bhauma-Karas of Orissa*, Ch.III.

104. Bhagvanlal Indraji and G. Bühler, 'Inscriptions from Nepal', *IA*, IX, 1880, pp. 163-94.

105. माद्यद्दन्तिसमूहदन्तमुसलक्षुण्णारिभूभृच्छिरो
गौडोड्रादिकलिङ्गकोसलपतिश्रीहर्षदेवात्मजा।
देवी राज्यमती कुलोचितगुणैर्युक्ता प्रभूता कुलै-
र्येनोढा भगदत्तराजकुलजा लक्ष्मीरिव क्ष्माभुजा।।
Ibid., verse 15.

Pl. I. Temple No. 1, North Gateway

Pl. II. *Yoni*

Pl. III. Gaṇeśa: four-armed, seated, in a niche

Pl. IV. Gaṇeśa: four-armed, seated

Pl. I. Temple No. 1, North Gateway

Pl. II. *Yoni*

Pl. III. Gaṇeśa: four-armed, seated, in a niche

Pl. IV. Gaṇeśa: four-armed, seated

Pl. V. Śiva: three-eyed, four-armed

Pl. VI. Uma-Maheśvara: upper part broken

Pl. VII. Kālī: strident

Pl. VIII. Kālī: seated

Pl. IX. Ugra-Tārā: upper part

Pl. X. Ugra-Tārā

Pl. XI. Vaishṇavī: upper part broken

Pl. XII. Dancing Śaiva ascetic

Pl. XIII. Ascetic observing penance: upper part

Pl. XIV. Female figure in *tribhaṅga*, upper part broken

Pl. XV. Nartakī (female danseuse)

Pl. XVI. Nartakī

Pl. XVII. Vidyādhara

Pl. XVIII. Mṛidaṅgavādinī

Pl. XIX. Sarasvatī

Pl. XX. Sarasvatī

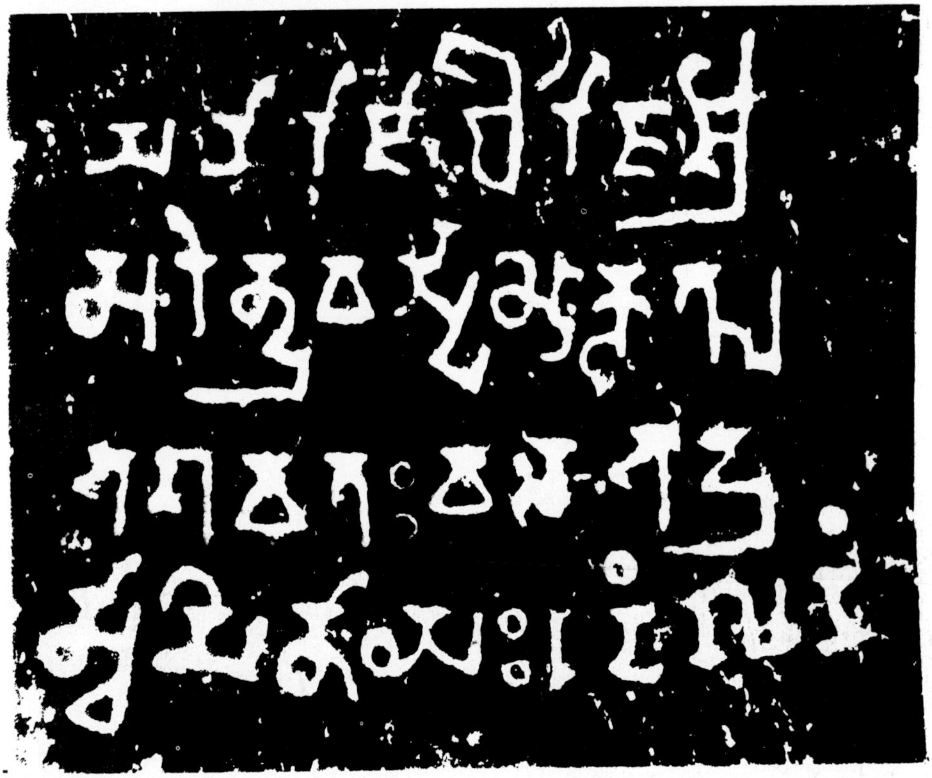

Pl. XXI. Umāchal Rock Inscription of Surendravarman

Pl. XXII. Baḍgaṅgā Rock Inscription of Bhūtivarman

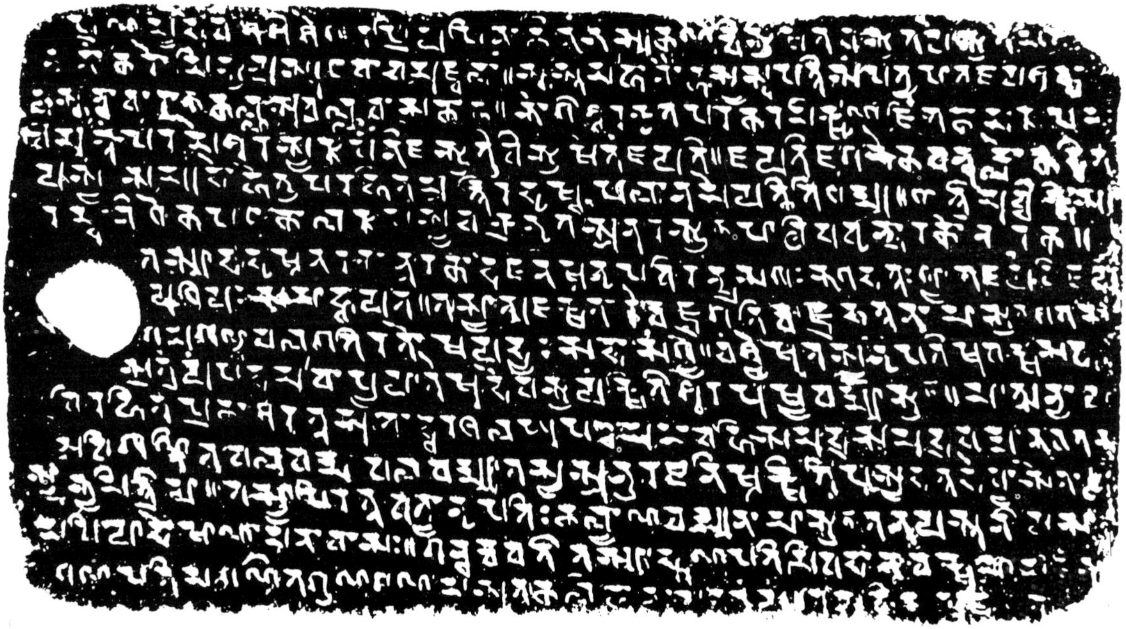

Pl. XXIII. Plate I

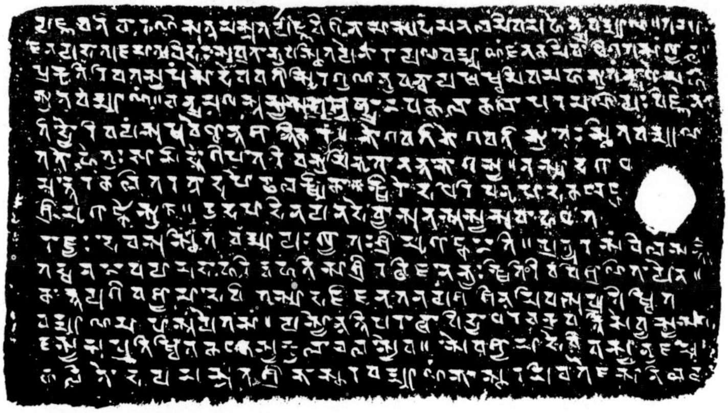

Pl. XXIV. Plate II, First Side

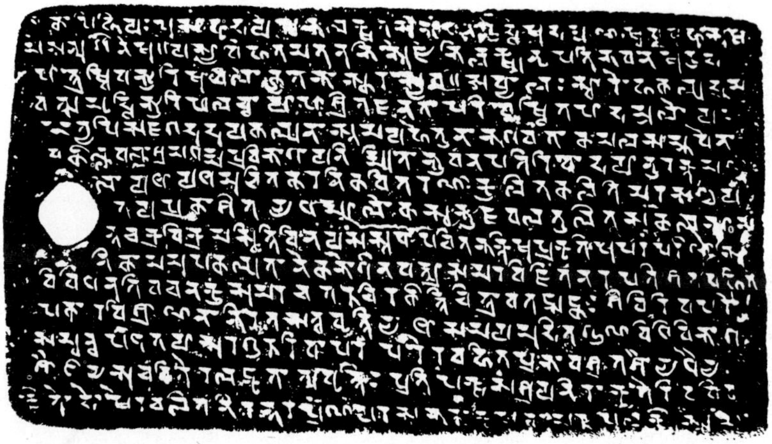

Pl. XXV. Plate II, Second Side

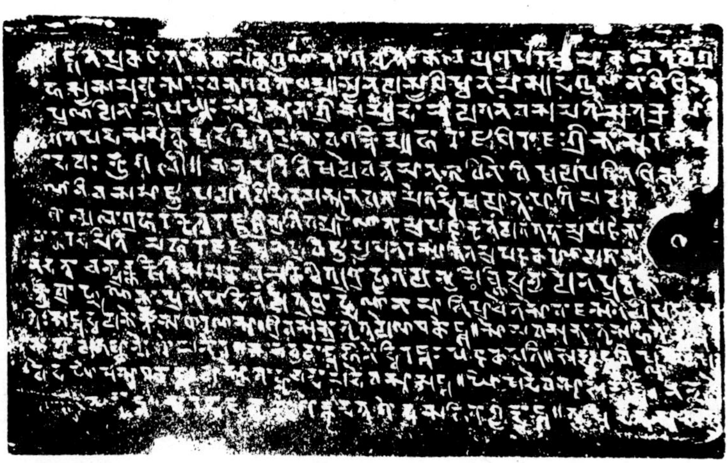

Pl. XXVI. Plate III, First Side

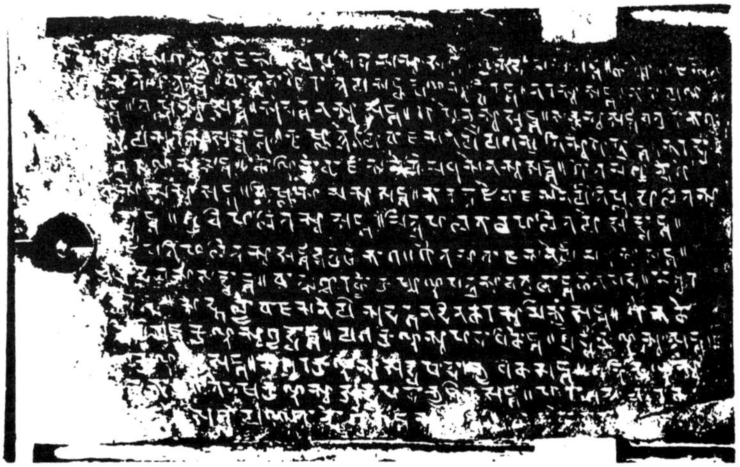

Pl. XXVII. Plate III, Second Side

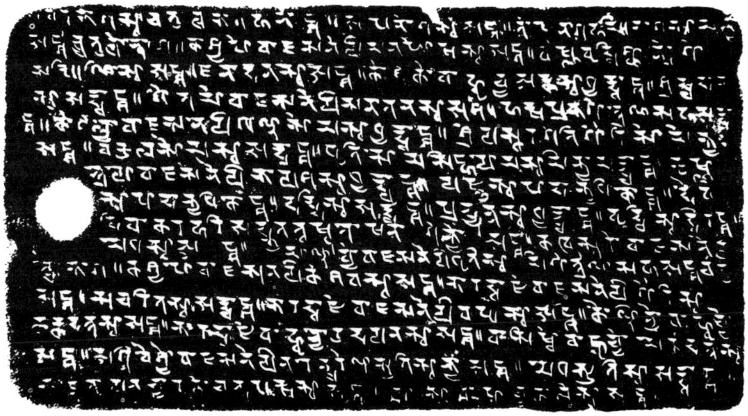

Pl. XXVIII. Plate IV, First Side

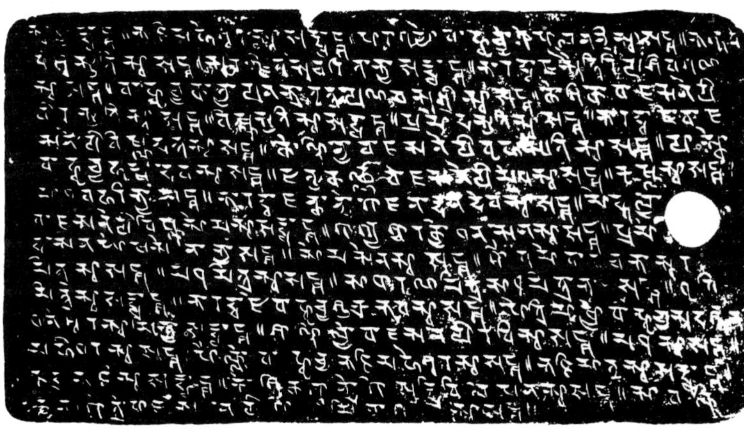

Pl. XXIX. Plate IV, Second Side

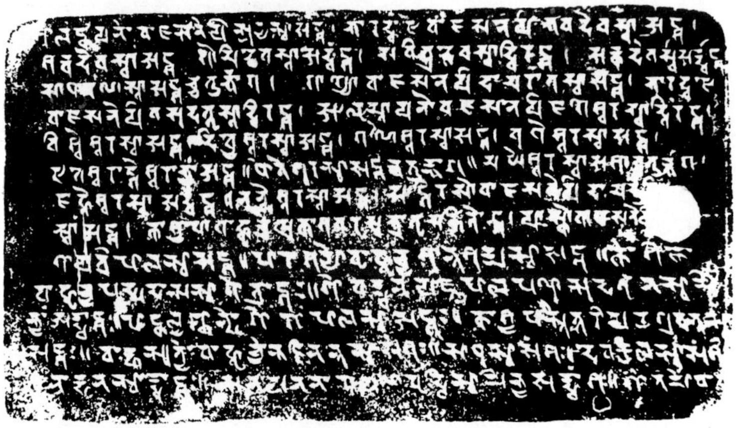

Pl. XXX. Plate V, First Side

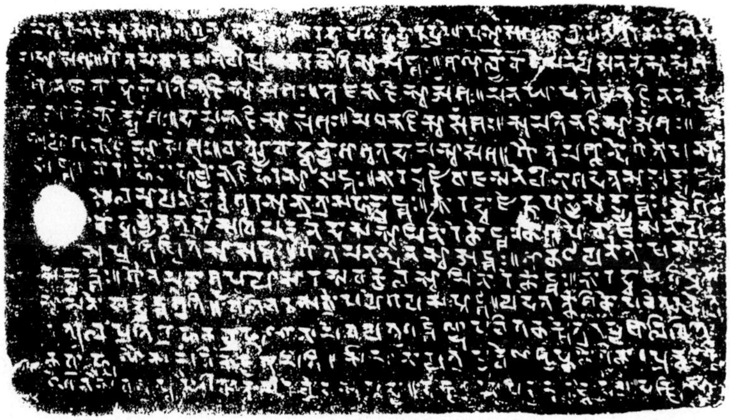

Pl. XXXI. Plate V, Second Side

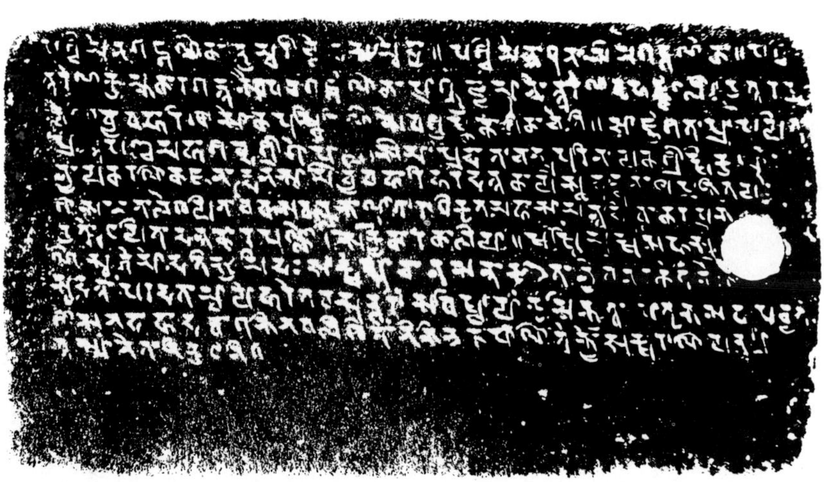

Pl. XXXII. Plate VI

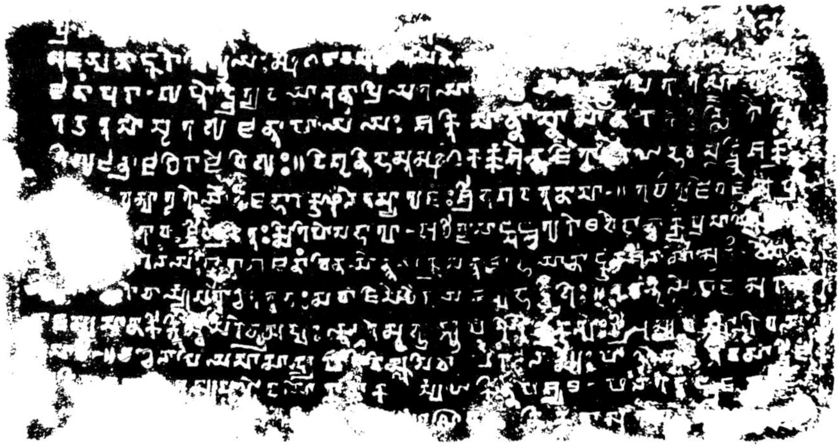

Pl. XXXIII. Plate I

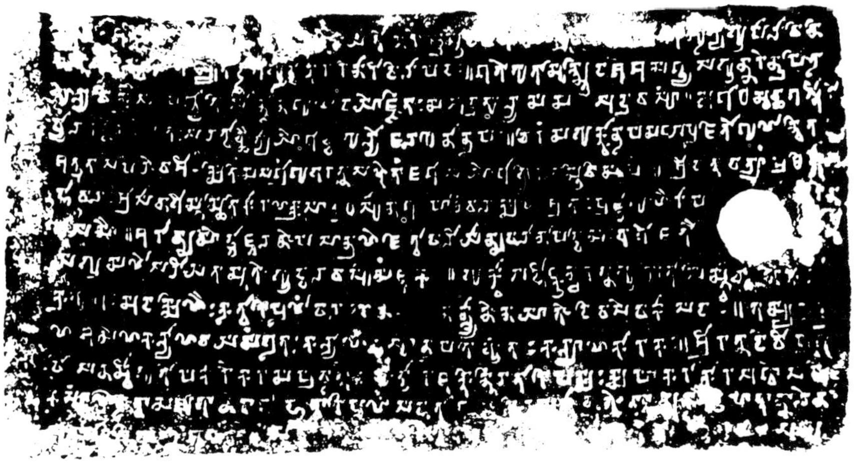

Pl. XXXIV. Plate II, First Side

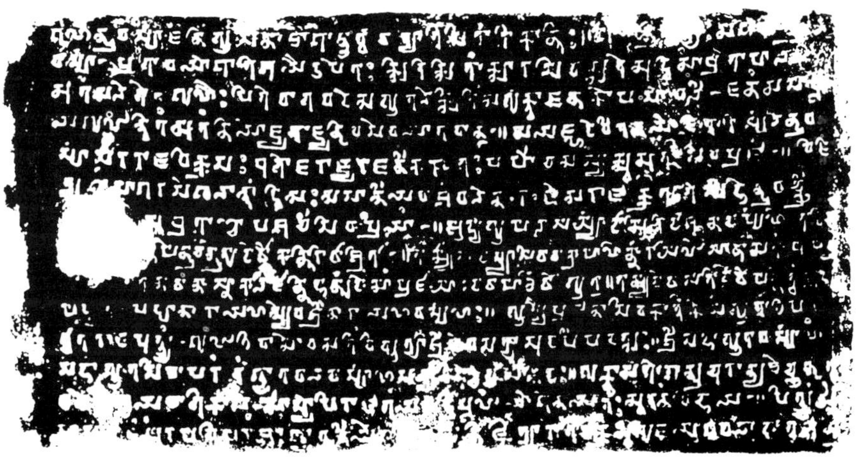

Pl. XXXV. Plate II, Second Side

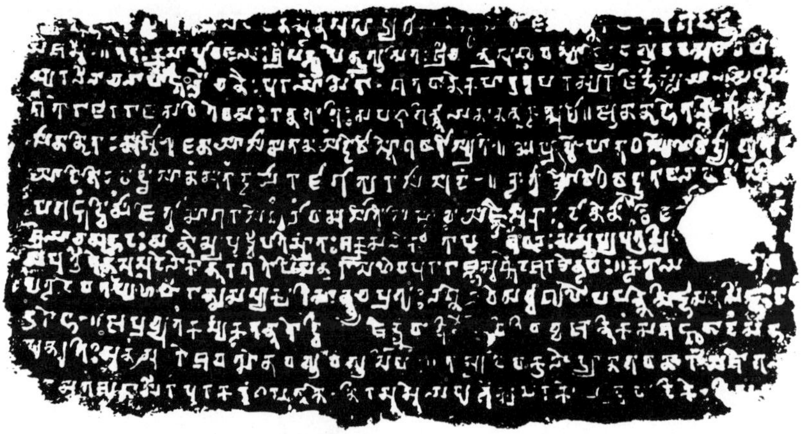

Pl. XXXVI. Plate III, First Side

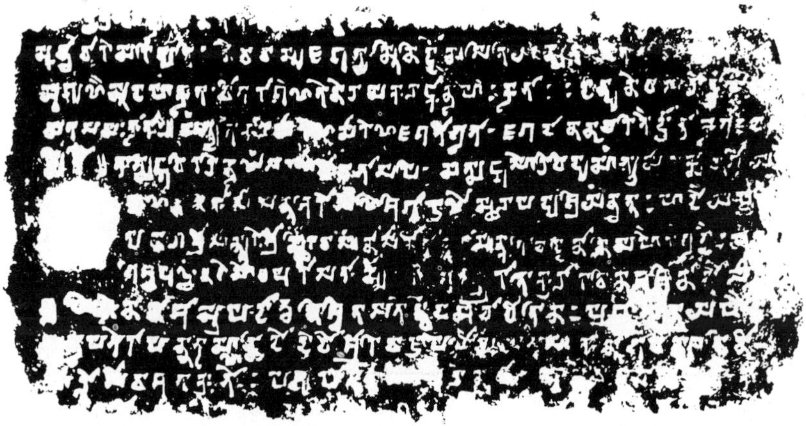

Pl. XXXVII. Plate III, Second Side

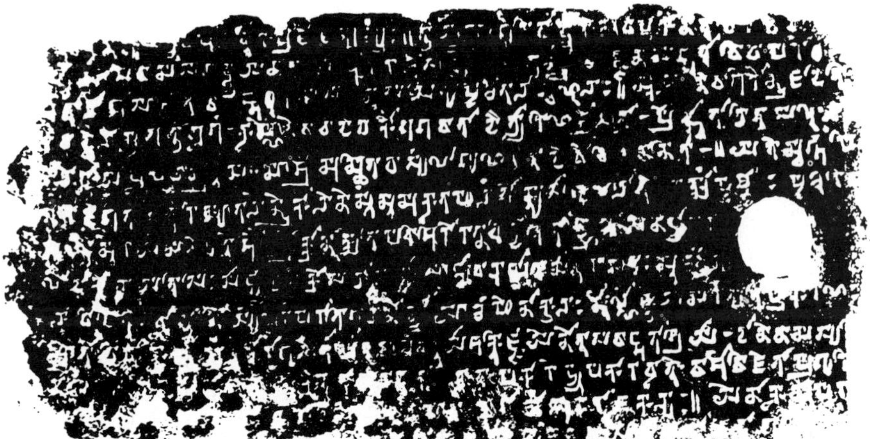

Pl. XXXVIII. Plate IV, First Side

Pl. XXXIX. Plate IV, Second Side

Pl. XL. Plate V, First Side

Pl. XLI. Plate V, Second Side

Pl. XLII. Dūbi Seal of Bhāskaravarman

Pl. XLIII. Nālandā Seals of Bhāskaravarman

SELECT BIBLIOGRAPHY

A. ORIGINAL SOURCES

I. Inscriptions

Banerji, R.D. : 'Neulpur Plate of Śubhākara: The 8th Year', *EL,* XV, 1919-20, pp. 1-8.

Basak, R.G. : 'The Five Dāmodarpur Copper-Plate Inscriptions of the Gupta Period', *ibid.,* pp. 113-45.

: 'Tipperah Copper-Plate Grant of Lokanātha, the 44th year', *ibid.,* pp. 301-15.

Bhandarkar, D.R. : 'A List of Inscriptions of Northern India in Brāhmi and its Derivative Scripts, from about 200 A. C.', Appendix to *EI,* XIX-XXII.

Bhandarkar, D.R. (reviser), Chhabra, B. Ch and Gai, G.S. (eds.) : *Inscriptions of the Early Gupta Kings, CII.* III, Archaeological Survey of India, New Delhi, 1981.

Bhattacharya, Padmanatha : *Kāmarūpa-śāsanāvalī* (Bengali), Rangapur Sahitya Parishat, Rangpur, 1931.

: 'Nidhānpur Copper-Plates of Bhāskaravarman', *EI,* XI, 1913-14, pp. 65-79; 'Two Lost Plates of Nidhānpur Copper-Plates of Bhāskaravarman', *ibid.,* XIX, 1927-28, pp. 115-27; 'A Third Lost Plate of the Nīdhānpur Plates of Bhāskara-varman', *ibid.,* pp. 245-50.

Bhattasali, N.K. : 'Baḍagangā Rock Inscription of Bhūtivarman', *ibid.,* XXVIII, 1947-48, pp. 18-23.

Fleet, J.F. : *Inscriptions of the Early Gupta Kings and their Successors, CII.* III, Calcutta, 1888.

Gupta, K.K. : *Copper-Plates of Sylhet.*

Hültzsch, E. : 'Plates of the Time of Śaśāṅkarāja, Gupta Saṁvat 300', *EI,* VI, 1900-1901, pp. 143-46.

Indraji, Bhagvanlal, and Bühler, G. : 'Inscriptions from Nepal', *IA,* IX, 1880, pp. 163-94.

Kielhorn, F. : 'Khalimpur Plate of Dharmapāla', *EL,* IV, 1896-97, pp. 253-54.

Majumdar, R.C. : 'Two Copper-Plates of Śaśāṅka from Midna-pore'. *JRASBL,* XI 1945, pp. 1-9

Misra, Binayak : 'Hindol Plate of Śubhākaradeva', *JBORS,* XVI, 1930 pp. 69-83.

Ramesh, K.V. and Tewari, S.P. : *A Copper-Plate Hoard of the Gupta Period from Bāgh, Madhya Pradesh,* Archaeological Survey of India, New Delhi, 1990.

Sarma, Dimbeshwar : *Kāmarūpa-śāsanāvalī,* Publication Board, Assam, Guwahati, 1981.

Sastri, Hirananda : *Nālandā and its Epigraphical Material, Memoirs of the Archaeological Survey of India,* No. 66, New Delhi, 1942.

Sharma, M.M. : *Inscriptions of Ancient Assam,* University of Gauhati, 1971.

Sircar, D.C. : 'Note on Baḍgaṅgā Inscription of Bhūtivarman', *EI.,* XXX, 1953-54, pp. 62-67.

: 'Dūbi Plates of Bhāskaravarman', *ibid.* XXX, 1953-54, pp. 287-304.

: *Indian Epigraphical Glossary,* Motilal Banarsidass, Delhi, 1966.

Sircar, D.C. and Choudhury, P.D. : 'Umāchal Rock Inscription of Surendravarman', *EI.,* XXXI, 1955-56, pp. 67-69.

Tripathi, Narayan : 'Chaurāsī Grant of Śivakaradeva', *JBORS,* XIV, 1929, pp. 292-306.

Venice, Arthur : 'Copper-Plate Grant of Vaidyadeva, a King of Kāmarūpa', *EI.,* II, 1894, pp. 347-58.

II. Sanskrit Literature

: *Ārya-Mañjuśrī-mūla-kalpa,* ed. T. Ganapati Sastri, 3 parts, Trivandrum Sanskrit Series, 1920-25; also in Jayaswal, K.P., *Imperial History of India,* Lahore, 1934.

: *Harivaṁśa-purāṇa,* with a Hindi translation by R.N. Shastri Pandeya, Gita Press, Gorakhpur (date not mentioned)

: *Kālikā-purāṇa,* Venkateswar Press, Mumbai, Śaka 1829.

: *Mārkaṇḍeya-purāṇa,* English translation by F.E. Pargiter, Calcutta, 1904.

: *Māhābhārata,* Gita Press edn., 4 vols., Gorakhpur, Vikrama Saṁvat 2013-15. See also *Mahābhārata kī Nāmānukramaṇikā* (Hindi), Gita Press, Gorakhpur, Vikrama Saṁvat 2016.

: *Rāmāyaṇa* of Vālmīki, with Tilaka, Śiromaṇi and Bhūshaṇa commentaries, 7 vols, Mumbai, 1912-18.

: *Yogini-tantra.*

Amarasiṁha : *Amarakosha* with Rāmāśramī commentary of Bhānujidīkshita, Nirnaya Sagar Press, Mumbai, 1944.

Bāṇabhaṭṭa : *Harsha-charita,* with Śaṅkara's Saṅketa commentary, ed. A.A. Führer, Bombay Sanskrit Series, No. LXVI, Mumbai, 1909.

Kalhaṇa : *Rāja-taraṅgiṇī,* ed. M.A. Stein, Reprint, Motilal

Banarisidass, Delhi, 1960; English translation by M.A. Stein, London, 1900; Reprint, 2 vols., Motilal Banarsidass, Delhi, 1961; Engl. tr. by R.S. Pandit, Allahabad, 1935; text with Hindi translation by Ramtej Shastri Pandeya, Pandit Pustakalaya, Varanasi, 1960.

Kālidāsa : *Raghuvaṁśa,* in Reva Prasad Dvivedi (ed.) *Kālidāsa-granthāvalī,* Banaras Hindu University, Varanasi, 1986, pp. 139-322.

: *Mālavikāgnimitra, ibid.,* pp. 323-432.

Kauṭilya : *Arthaśāsrā,* ed. M. Shamasastri, Government Oriental Institute, Mysore, 1919; ed. R.P. Kangle, University of Bombay, 1960; Engl. tr. Shamasastri, 3rd edn., Mysore, 1929; Engl. tr. by Kangle, Mumbai, 1963.

Pāṇini : *Ashtadjyāyī,* ed. Shankaradeva Pasthak, Gurukula Vṛindavan, Vikrama Saṁvat, 1999.

Pargiter, F.E. : *The Purāṇa Text of the Dynasties of the Kali Age,* Oxford, 1913.

Viśākhadatta : *Mūdrārākshasa,* ed. with an Engl. tr. by K.H. Dhruva, Pune, 1923.

III. Non-Indian Sources

: *She-kia-fang-che,* Visva-Bharati, Shantiniketan.

Beal, Samuel : *The Life of Hiuen Tsiang* by Shaman Hwui Li, Academica Asiatica, Delhi, 1973.

Majumdar, R.C. (ed.) : *Classical Accounts of India,* Firma K.L. Mukhopadhyaya, Calcutta, 1960.

McCrindle, J.W. : *Ancient India as described in Classical Literature,* Westminster, 1910.

: *The Commerce and Navigation of the Erythraean Sea,* Calcutta, Mumbai, London, 1879.

Schoff, W.H. : 'Anonymi (Ut Fertur) Periplus Maris Eryrthaei', *IA,* VIII, 1879, pp. 107-51.

: *The Periplus of the Erythraean Sea,* London, 1912.

Watters, Thomas : *On Yuan Chwang's Travels in India,* 2 vols., posthumously revised by T.W. Rhys Davids and S.W. Bushell, Royal Asiatic Society, London, 1904-05.

B. MODERN WRITINGS

Agrawal, D.P. : *Archaeology of India,* Curzon Press, London and Malmö, 1982.

Agrawala, V.S. : *Harsha-charita: Eka Saṁskṛitika Adhyayana* (Hindi), Bihar Rashtrabhasha Parishad, Patna, 1953.

: *India as known to Pāṇini,* 2nd edn., Prithivi Prakashan, Varanasi, 1963.

Ansari, Mohammad Azhar : *Geographical Glimpses of Medieval India,* II, Delhi, 1984.

Baden-Powell : *The Indian Village Community,* London, 1897.

Bagchi, P.C. (ed.) : *India and China,* Calcutta, 1944.
: *Pre-Aryan and Pre-Dravidian in India,* 1929.

Bamzai, P.N.K. : *A History of Kashmir: Political, Social and Cultural,* 2nd edn., Metropolitan Book Company, Delhi, 1973.

Barua, B.K. : *A Cultural History of Assam,* Part I: Early Period, Nowgong, 1951.

Barua, K.L. : *Early History of Kāmarūpa,* Shillong, 1933.
: *Studies in the Early History of Assam,* ed. Maheshwar Neog, Asam Sahitya Sabha, Jorhat-Guwahati, 1973.

Basak, R.G. : *History of North-Eastern India,* Calcutta, 1934.

Bhandarkar, D.R. : 'The Nāgar Brāhmaṇas and the Bengal Kāyasthas', *IA,* LXI, 1932, pp. 41-59, 61-72.

Bhattacharya, B. : 'The Tibetan Translation of the Sādhanamālā: A Rejoinder', *IHQ,* III, 1927, pp. 419-28.

Bhattacharya, N.N. : *Religious Culture of North-Eastern India,* Manohar Publications, New Delhi, 1995.

Bhattasali, N.K. : 'New Light on the History of Assam,' *IHQ,* XXI, 1945, pp. 19-28.

Chatterji, S.K. : *Origin and Development of Bengali Language,* Calcutta, 1926.

——— : *Kirāta-jana-kṛiti: The Indo-Mongoloids: Their Contribution to the History and Culture of India,* 2nd edn, Asiatic Society, Calcutta, 1974.

——— : *Indo-Aryan and Hindi,* Calcutta, 1942.

Chattopadhyaya, Sudhakara : *Early History of Northern India,* 2nd edn., Academic Publishers, Calcutta, 1968.

Choudhury, P.C. : *The History of the Civilisation of the People of Assam to the Twelfth Century AD,* Dept. of Historical and Antiquarian Studies in Assam, Guwahati, 1978.

Cribb, Joe : 'Numismatic Evidence for the Date of the "Periplus", *Numismatics, History, Art & Culture: Essays in Honour of Dr. Parmeshwarilal Gupta,* eds. D.W. Macdowall, Savita Sharma and Sanjay Garg, Agam Kala Prakashan, Delhi, 1992.

Dange, S.A. : *Cultural Sources from the Veda,* Bharatiya Vidya Bhavan, Mumbai, 1977.

Deo, S.B. and Kamath, S.U. (eds.) : *The Āryan Problem,* Bhāratīya Itihāsa Saṅkalana Samiti, Pune, 1993.

Devendra Swarup : 'Genesis of the Āryan Race Theory and its Application to Indian History', in Deo and Kamath (eds.), *ibid.,* pp. 30-39.

Dikshitar, V.R.R. : 'Aryanisation of East India (Assam)', *IHQ,* XXI, 1945, pp. 29-33.

Gait, E.A. : *A History of Assam,* 2nd edn., Calcutta, 1925.

Ganguly, D.C. : 'Political Condition of Bengal during Hiuen Tsang's Visit', *IHQ,* XV, 1939, pp. 122-26.

Ghosh, J.C. : 'Grant of Bhāskara Varmā of Kāmarūpa and the Nāgara Brāhmaṇas', *ibid.*, VI, 1930, pp. 60-71.

Gogoi, Pushpadhar : *The Tai of North-East India*, Dhemji, 1996.

Grierson, A.A. : *Linguistic Survey of India*, II.

Gupta, K.M. : 'Identification of Brahmottara', *IHQ*, VII, 1931, pp. 743-46.

Gupta, S.P. : *Indus-Saraswatī Civilization*, Pratibha Prakashan, Delhi, 1997.

Gupta, S.P. and Ramachandran K.S. (eds.) : *Mahābhārata: Myth and Reality: Differing Views*, Agam Prakashan, Delhi, 1976.

Jain, J.C. : *Life in Ancient India as Depicted in the Jain Canon*, Mumbai, 1947.

Kakati, B.K. (ed.) : *The Mother Goddess Kāmākhyā*, Guwahati, 1943.

——— : *Assamese — Its Formation and Development*, Guwahati, 1941.

——— : *Aspects of Early Assamess Literature*, University of Gauhati, 1953.

Kane, P.V. : *History of Dharmaśāstra*, III, Bhandarkar Oriental Research Institute, Pune, 1946.

Lal, B.B. : 'Excavations at Hastinapur and Other Exploration in Upper Ganga and Sutlej Basin: 1950-52', *Ancient India*, Nos. 11-12, 1954-55, pp. 1-151.

Max Müller, F. : *Selected Essays on Language, Mythology and Religion*, I, London, 1881.

Majumdar, R.C. : 'The Extent of Harshavardhana's Empire', *IHQ*, V, 1929, pp. 228-36.

: *History of Bengal*, I, Dacca University, 1943.

Majumdar, R.C. and Pusalkar, A.D. (eds.) : *The History and Culture of the Indian People*, III: *The Classical Age*, Bharatiya Vidya Bhavan, Mumbai, 1954.

Momin, Mignonette : 'Studies in Political and Socio-Economic History of Pre-Ahom Assam: Perspectives and Prospects', *North-Eastern Hill University Journal of Social Sciences and Humanities*, I (I), January-July 1998, pp. 1-20.

Motichandra : *Sārthavāha* (Hindi), Bihar Rashtrabhasha Parishad, Patna, 1966.

: *Trade and Trade Routes in Ancient India*, Abhinav Publications, New Delhi, 1977.

Nath, R.M. : *The Background of Assamese Culture*, Shillong, 1948.

Pargiter, F.E. : 'Ancient Countries in Eastern India', *JASB*, 1897.

: *Ancient Indian Historical Tradition*, London, 1922.

Pathak, V.S. : 'Semantics of Ārya: Its Historical Implications', in The *Āryan Problem*, eds. S.B. Deo and S.U. Kamath, pp. 86-99.

Pauthier, M. : 'Thien-chu - India: Extract from Ma-twan-lin, Book CCCXXXVIII, Fol. 14', *IA*, 1880, pp. 14-23.

Ray, N.R. : 'Harsha-Śīlāditya: A Revised Study', *IHQ*, III, 1927, pp. 763-93.

Ray, Sunil Chandra : *Early History and Culture of Kashmir,* Calcutta, 1957.

Roy, S.B. : *Date of the Mahābhārata War,* The Academic Press, Gurgaon, 1976.

Sengupta, P.C. : 'Astronomical References in the Mahābhārata and their Significance', *JRASBL,* III, 1933, pp. 101-19.

——— : 'Bhārata Battle Traditions', *ibid.,* IV, 1935, 395-413.

Sharma, A.K. : *Emergence of Early Culture in North-East India (A study based on excavations at Bhaitbari, Meghalaya),* Aryan Books International, New Delhi, 1993.

: *Manipur: The Glorious Past,* Aryan Books International, New Delhi, 1994.

Shastri, Ajay Mitra : *India as seen in the Kuṭṭanī-mata* of *Dāmodragupta,* Motilal Banarsidass, Delhi, 1975.

: *Varāhamihira's India,* 2 vols., Aryan Books International, New Delhi, 1996.

: *Varāhamihira and his Times,* Kusumanjali Prakashan, Jodhpur, 1991.

: 'Āryāvarta and Jambūdvīpa', in Deo and Kamath (eds.), *The Āryan Problem,* pp. 135-42.

: 'The Indus Civilization and the So-called Aryans', *Saṁskṛiti Sandhāna,* IV, 1991, pp. 64-70.

: 'Fresh light in the History of Prāgyotisha: Pushyavarman was son of Naraka', *JARS,* XXXV, 1995, pp. 32-35.

: *The Sātavāhanas and the Western Kshatrāpas: A Historical Framework,* Dattsons, Nagpur, 1998.

: 'Seals of Bhāskaravarman: Some Reflections', *Studies in Indian Epigraphy (Bhāratīya Purābhilekha Patrikā),* XXVI, 2000, pp. 20-32.

: (ed.) *Mahābhārata: Some Facets,* under publication by Indian Institute of Advanced Study, Shimla.

: 'Prāgyotisha in Mahābhārata', in *ibid.,*

Singh, Bhagwan : 'Trade and Commerce in the Vedic Age', in Deo and Kamath (eds.), *The Āryan Problem,* pp. 192-200.

: *The Vedic Harappans,* Aditya Prakashan, New Delhi, 1995.

Singh, Jai Prakash : 'Was Bhāskaravarman a Feudatory'?, *Journal of the North-East India Council of Social Science Research,* XXII (II), Oct. 1998, pp. 5-10.

Singh, Jai Prakash and Sengupta, Gautam (eds.) : *Archaeology of North-Eastern India,* Har-Anand and Vikas Publications, New Delhi, 1991.

Sinha, B.P. : *The Decline of the Kingdom of Magadha*, Patna, 1954.

Sircar, D.C. : 'Aśvamedhas Celebrated by Kāmarūpa Kings', *IHQ,* XXI, 1945,p p. 143-45.

Sircar, D.C. : 'Gauḍa-Kāmarūpa Struggle in the 6th-7th Centuries AD', *ibid.*, XXVI, 1950, pp. 241-46.

——— : *Studies in the Geography of Ancient and Mediaeval India*, 2nd edn., Motilal Banarsidass, Delhi, 1972.

Spooner, D.B. : 'The Zoroastrian Background of Indian History', *JRAS*, 1915, pp. 433-36.

Sudhi, Umakanta : *The Bhauma-Karas of Orissa*, Punthi Pustak, Calcutta, 1975.

Tripathi, R.S. : *History of Kanauj*, Varanasi, 1937.

Tripathi, Vibha : *The Painted Grey Ware: An Iron Age Culture of Northern India*, Concept Publishing Company, Delhi, 1975.

INDEX*

*** Notes and References have not been indexed.**

The following abbreviations have been employed in this Index:-
a.=author, *ad.*=admnistrative division, *c.*=country, *d.*=dynasty, *g.*=gotra, *k.*=king, *l.*=locality, *m.*=mountain, *p.*=people, *q.*=queen, *r.*=river, *t.*=text.